Workbook

Science

PEARSON
Scott Foresman

Editorial Offices: Glenview, Illinois • Parsippany, New Jersey • New York, New York
Sales Offices: Needham, Massachusetts • Duluth, Georgia • Glenview, Illinois
Coppell, Texas • Sacramento, California • Mesa, Arizona

www.sfsuccessnet.com

Series Authors

Dr. Timothy Cooney
Professor of Earth Science and
Science Education
University of Northern Iowa (UNI)
Cedar Falls, Iowa

Dr. Jim Cummins
Professor
Department of Curriculum,
Teaching, and Learning
The University of Toronto
Toronto, Canada

Dr. James Flood
Distinguished Professor of Literacy
and Language
School of Teacher Education
San Diego State University
San Diego, California

Barbara Kay Foots, M.Ed.
Science Education Consultant
Houston, Texas

Dr. M. Jenice Goldston
Associate Professor of Science
Education
Department of Elementary Education
Programs
University of Alabama
Tuscaloosa, Alabama

Dr. Shirley Gholston Key
Associate Professor of Science
Education
Instruction and Curriculum Leadership
Department
College of Education
University of Memphis
Memphis, Tennessee

Dr. Diane Lapp
Distinguished Professor of Reading
and Language Arts in Teacher
Education
San Diego State University
San Diego, California

Sheryl A. Mercier
Classroom Teacher
Dunlap Elementary School
Dunlap, California

Dr. Karen L. Ostlund
UTeach, College of Natural Sciences
The University of Texas at Austin
Austin, Texas

Dr. Nancy Romance
Professor of Science Education
& Principal Investigator
NSF/IERI Science IDEAS Project
Charles E. Schmidt College
of Science
Florida Atlantic University
Boca Raton, Florida

Dr. William Tate
Chair and Professor of Education
and Applied Statistics
Department of Education
Washington University
St. Louis, Missouri

Dr. Kathryn C. Thornton
Professor
School of Engineering and
Applied Science
University of Virginia
Charlottesville, Virginia

Dr. Leon Ukens
Professor of Science Education
Department of Physics, Astronomy,
and Geosciences
Towson University
Towson, Maryland

Steve Weinberg
Consultant
Connecticut Center for
Advanced Technology
East Hartford, Connecticut

Consulting Author

Dr. Michael P. Klentschy
Superintendent
El Centro Elementary School District
El Centro, California

ISBN: 0-328-12613-6

ISBN: 0-328-20067-0

11 12 13 14 15 16 V084 10 09 08 07

© Pearson Education, Inc.

Unit A
Life Science

Unit B
Earth Science

Unit C
Physical Science

Unit D
Space and Technology

Name _____

The Personal Vocabulary Journal shows vocabulary words you will see in this chapter as well as a sentence using each word. Use clues from each sentence to help you predict the meaning of the vocabulary word.

Personal Vocabulary Journal		
Vocabulary word	**Word used in a sentence**	**What I think the word means**
cell	All living things are made of **cells**.	
nucleus	All cells have a **nucleus** at their center.	
cytoplasm	Without **cytoplasm**, cells could not carry out their life processes.	
chloroplast	Only plant cells have **chloroplasts**.	
genus	Wolves and dogs belong to the same **genus**.	
species	Wolves and dogs belong to different **species**.	
vertebrates	All mammals, fishes, amphibians, reptiles, and birds are **vertebrates**.	
invertebrates	Jellyfish, worms, snails, and clams are examples of **invertebrates**.	

 Notes for Home: Your child learned the vocabulary terms for Chapter 1.
Home Activity: Look through pictures of animals with your child and use the terms *genus, species, vertebrate,* and *invertebrate* to classify the animals.

Name _____

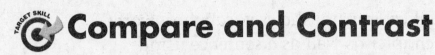

Compare and Contrast

A science class was asked to read about moss and bamboo and then record several characteristics of each type of plant. One student's record is shown below.

Characteristics of Bamboo and Moss

Bamboo plants grow very tall. They have leaves, roots, and stems. They are a vascular plant. Bamboo plants can make their own food. Bamboo cells contain chloroplasts. Mosses are nonvascular plants. They do not have leaves or stems. They are able to make their own food. Moss cells contain chloroplasts.

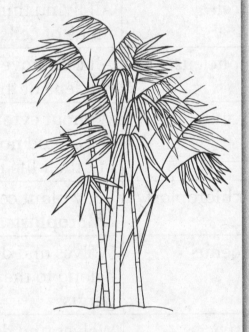

Apply It!

Fill in the graphic organizer on the next page. Write the characteristics of bamboo in one circle. Write the characteristics of moss in the other circle. Write any characteristics that bamboo and moss have in common in the center section.

Bamboo   **Both**   **Moss**

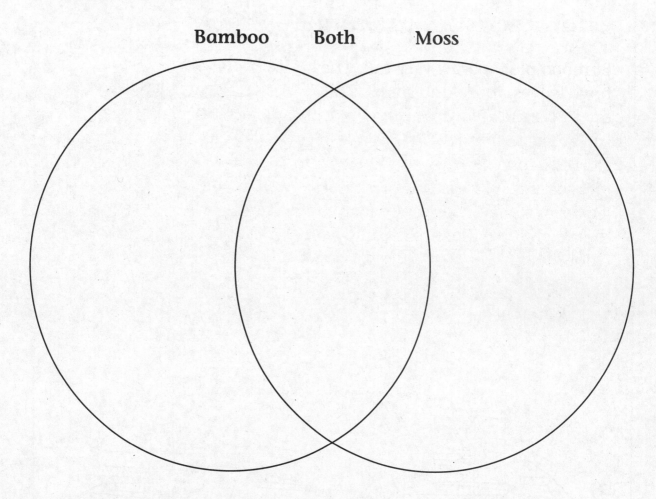

Notes for Home: Your child learned how to compare and contrast two organisms.
Home Activity: Have your child choose two animals. Together make a graphic organizer like the one above and use it to compare and contrast the characteristics of the animals.

Notes

Lesson 1: What are the building blocks of life?

Before You Read Lesson 1

Read each statement below. Place a check mark in the circle to indicate whether you agree or disagree with the statement.

		Agree	Disagree
1.	All living things are made of millions of cells.	○	○
2.	The heart is a muscle.	○	○
3.	A virus is a cell that makes its own food.	○	○
4.	Plants cells and animal cells are both made up of the same parts.	○	○

After You Read Lesson 1

Reread each statement above. If the lesson supports your choice, place a check mark in the *Correct* circle. Then explain how the text supports your choice. If the lesson does not support your choice, place a check mark in the *Incorrect* circle. Then explain why your choice is wrong.

		Correct	Incorrect
1.	_____	○	○
	_____		
2.	_____	○	○
	_____		
3.	_____	○	○
	_____		
4.	_____	○	○
	_____		

Notes for Home: Your child has completed a pre/post inventory of key concepts in the lesson.
Home Activity: Have your child compare and contrast animal cells and plant cells.

Reviewing Terms: Matching

Match each description with the correct word. Write the letter on the line next to each description.

_____ 1. the control center of a cell

_____ 2. the smallest unit of a living thing that performs all life processes

_____ 3. the gel-like liquid in a cell

_____ 4. the cell part that traps the Sun's energy

a. cell

b. chloroplast

c. nucleus

d. cytoplasm

Reviewing Concepts: Sentence Completion

Complete each sentence with the correct word or phrase.

_____ 5. A microscope makes cells look _____ so that they can be studied. (smaller, larger)

_____ 6. A cell's _____ separates it from its environment. (membrane, nucleus)

_____ 7. A tissue is made up of _____. (organs, cells)

_____ 8. A _____ is a cell part that only plants have. (nucleus, cell wall)

Applying Strategies: Main Idea and Supporting Details

Use complete sentences to answer question 9. (2 points)

9. On the lines below, write three details that support the main idea.

   Main Idea: Cells are the building blocks of life.

   Detail:_____

   Detail:_____

   Detail:_____

   _____

Lesson 2: How are living things grouped?

Before You Read Lesson 2

Read each statement below. Place a check mark in the circle to indicate whether you agree or disagree with the statement.

		Agree	Disagree
1.	Scientists group living things by how they get food.	○	○
2.	All plants make their own food.	○	○
3.	The largest classification group is a species.	○	○
4.	The first part of an organism's scientific name is its genus.	○	○

After You Read Lesson 2

Reread each statement above. If the lesson supports your choice, place a check mark in the *Correct* circle. Then explain how the text supports your choice. If the lesson does not support your choice, place a check mark in the *Incorrect* circle. Then explain why your choice is wrong.

		Correct	Incorrect
1.	_____ _____	○	○
2.	_____ _____	○	○
3.	_____ _____	○	○
4.	_____ _____	○	○

© Pearson Education, Inc.

Notes for Home: Your child has completed a pre/post inventory of key concepts in the lesson.
Home Activity: Have your child classify a variety of living organisms by how many cells they have, where they live, and how they get food.

Reviewing Terms: Matching

Match each description with the correct word. Write the letter on the line next to each description.

_____ 1. a group of similar organisms that can mate and produce offspring

_____ 2. a group of closely related living things

a. genus

b. species

Reviewing Concepts: Matching

Match each kingdom in the right column with the best description in the left column. Write the letter on the line next to each description.

_____ 3. many of these organisms live in extremely hot or salty water

_____ 4. one-celled organisms with no separate nucleus

_____ 5. algae, amebas, and paramecia

_____ 6. includes mushrooms, yeast, and fungi

_____ 7. many-celled organisms that make their own food

_____ 8. many-celled organisms with organ systems that do not make their own food

a. Plants

b. Ancient Bacteria

c. Fungi

d. Animals

e. True Bacteria

f. Protists

Writing

Use complete sentences to answer question 9. (2 points)

9. Describe a characteristic of an organism that could help you determine to which kingdom the organism belongs.

_____

_____

_____

Lesson 3: How are plants classified?

Before You Read Lesson 3

Read each statement below. Place a check mark in the circle to indicate whether you agree or disagree with the statement.

		Agree	Disagree
1.	Leaves, stems, and roots are a plant's organs.	○	○
2.	All plants have tubes that move water and nutrients to all of their organs.	○	○
3.	Not all plants reproduce by seeds.	○	○
4.	Plants that make seeds also make flowers.	○	○

After You Read Lesson 3

Reread each statement above. If the lesson supports your choice, place a check mark in the *Correct* circle. Then explain how the text supports your choice. If the lesson does not support your choice, place a check mark in the *Incorrect* circle. Then explain why your choice is wrong.

		Correct	Incorrect
1.	_____	○	○
	_____		
2.	_____	○	○
	_____		
3.	_____	○	○
	_____		
4.	_____	○	○
	_____		

Notes for Home: Your child has completed a pre/post inventory of key concepts in the lesson.
Home Activity: Examine plants found around your home or neighborhood and have your child classify them according to a variety of characteristics.

Name _____

Reviewing Concepts: True or False

Write **T** (True) or **F** (False) on the line before each statement.

_____ 1. Plants with tubes to move water and nutrients are called vascular plants.

_____ 2. Vascular plants can grow taller than nonvascular plants.

_____ 3. Most nonvascular plants live in dry places.

_____ 4. Mosses do not have true stems or leaves.

_____ 5. Hornworts and liverworts are vascular plants.

_____ 6. Seeds have young plants and stored food inside them.

_____ 7. Conifers are plants that grow flowers.

_____ 8. Ferns and mosses reproduce using spores.

Applying Strategies: Using Decimals

9. Tara's class went on a field trip to a state forest. Of the trees they observed, $\frac{7}{10}$ reproduce using cones. Write a decimal that is equivalent to $\frac{7}{10}$. (2 points)

© Pearson Education, Inc.

Lesson 4: How are animals classified?

Before You Read Lesson 4

Read each statement below. Place a check mark in the circle to indicate whether you agree or disagree with the statement.

	Agree	Disagree
1. Scientists divide vertebrates into two main groups.	○	○
2. All mammals use lungs to breathe.	○	○
3. All arthropods are invertebrates.	○	○
4. A spider is an insect.	○	○

After You Read Lesson 4

Reread each statement above. If the lesson supports your choice, place a check mark in the *Correct* circle. Then explain how the text supports your choice. If the lesson does not support your choice, place a check mark in the *Incorrect* circle. Then explain why your choice is wrong.

	Correct	Incorrect
1. _____	○	○
_____		
2. _____	○	○
_____		
3. _____	○	○
_____		
4. _____	○	○
_____		

 Notes for Home: Your child has completed a pre/post inventory of key concepts in the lesson.
Home Activity: Brainstorm a list of animals and have your child place each animal into as many of the groups mentioned in the text as possible.

Reviewing Terms: Matching

Match each description with the correct word. Write the letter on the line next to each description.

_____ 1. animals with backbones

_____ 2. animals without backbones

a. invertebrates

b. vertebrates

Reviewing Concepts: Sentence Completion

Complete each sentence with the correct word.

_____ 3. _____ are a type of vertebrate with scales that live only in water. (Reptiles, Fish)

_____ 4. Warm-blooded vertebrates with hair or fur are called _____. (mammals, birds)

_____ 5. Alligators and crocodiles are examples of _____. (reptiles, amphibians)

_____ 6. Most of the animals in the world are _____. (vertebrates, invertebrates)

_____ 7. Insects, spiders, and crabs are _____. (arthropods, sponges)

_____ 8. Snails are _____. (mollusks, amphibians)

Applying Strategies: Sequence

9. Some of the steps in the life of a Burmese python are listed below, but they are out of order. Use the clue words to write the sentences in the correct order. (2 points)

First, the mother python lays eggs.
Finally, the mother python leaves and the young care for themselves.
Next, the mother python keeps the eggs warm.
Then the eggs hatch.

_____

_____

_____

Name _____

Lesson 5: How do animals adapt?

Before You Read Lesson 5

Read each statement below. Place a check mark in the circle to indicate whether you agree or disagree with the statement.

		Agree	Disagree
1.	Your hair color is a trait.	○	○
2.	The shape of a bird's beak is an adaptation.	○	○
3.	Migration is an adaptive behavior.	○	○
4.	Behaviors are either learned or they are inherited.	○	○

After You Read Lesson 5

Reread each statement above. If the lesson supports your choice, place a check mark in the *Correct* circle. Then explain how the text supports your choice. If the lesson does not support your choice, place a check mark in the *Incorrect* circle. Then explain why your choice is wrong.

		Correct	Incorrect
1.	_____	○	○
	_____		
2.	_____	○	○
	_____		
3.	_____	○	○
	_____		
4.	_____	○	○
	_____		

Notes for Home: Your child has completed a pre/post inventory of key concepts in the lesson.
Home Activity: Have your child explain how an animal's color is an adaptation that helps protect the animal.

© Pearson Education, Inc.

Reviewing Concepts: Matching

Animals' adaptations help them to survive. Some adaptations help animals get food. Other adaptations help animals avoid predators. Match each description in the left column with the way the adaptation helps the animal in the right column. You can use each answer more than once.

_____ 1. a box turtle's shell

_____ 2. a heron's long, sharp beak

_____ 3. a poison dart frog's bright colors

_____ 4. a giraffe's long neck

_____ 5. a rock ptarmigan's white winter feathers

_____ 6. a hummingbird's long, narrow beak

_____ 7. a Mandarin fish's bright colors

_____ 8. a crab-eating seal's teeth

a. an adaptation for getting food

b. an adaptation for avoiding predators

Applying Strategies: Compare and Contrast

Use complete sentences to answer question 9. (2 points)

9. Name one similarity between instincts and learned behavior. Describe one difference between them.

_____

_____

_____

_____

_____

Symmetry in Nature

Symmetry can be found in both animals and plants.

Decide whether or not these living things have symmetry.
Write *symmetry* or *no symmetry* on the line.

1.

2.

3.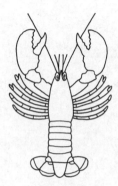

_____   _____   _____

Draw all lines of symmetry for these living things.

4.

5.

6.

 Notes for Home: Your child learned to recognize symmetry and lines of symmetry in plants and animals.
Home Activity: With your child, look at objects in and around your home and decide which have symmetry and how many lines of symmetry each symmetrical object has.

© Pearson Education, Inc.

Notes

Dear Family,

Your child is learning how scientists sort living things. In the science chapter Classifying Plants and Animals, our class has learned about the building blocks that make up all living things and how living things are named and grouped into six kingdoms. Students have also learned how to look for similarities and differences between living things; this will help them compare, contrast, and classify all kinds of organisms.

In addition to learning how to classify different kinds of living things, students have also learned many new vocabulary words. Help your child to make these words a part of his or her own vocabulary by using them when you talk together about plants and animals.

cell
nucleus
cytoplasm
chloroplast
genus
species
vertebrates
invertebrates

These following pages include activities that you and your child can do together. By participating in your child's education, you will help to bring the learning home.

Family Science Activity

Make a Collage of Living Things

Review how living things are classified. Make a colorful collage of different plants and animals.

Materials

- Magazines with pictures of different plants and animals
- Scissors
- Glue
- Pens, pencils, or markers
- Cardboard or construction paper

Steps

1. Find various pictures of mammals, birds, reptiles, amphibians, fish, and invertebrates.
2. Cut out the pictures. Glue them onto the cardboard or construction paper.
3. Label each picture. You can use the Internet or an encyclopedia to help you.

Talk About It

How many plants are in the collage?
How many kinds of animals are in the collage?
How many mammals are in the collage? reptiles? birds? invertebrates?
Why are cats, bears, monkeys, and humans all considered mammals?

Workbook

Vocabulary Practice

Find all of the vocabulary words from the Classifying Plants and Animals chapter in the word search below.

Classifying Living Things

```
V C H L O R O P L A S T K C D
L E J S Y B J Y N H Y D S Y M
P O R S U S B U J V E X T H
J L R T W N C W E U T D Q O S
F L Z W E L E X Y A D T Q P G
F E Q P E B P G R N E Z O L S
M C Q U E I R B I E L B Y A B
Y N S W R C E A D B G G K S I
K F J Y J T E G T O H L J M H
U A O E R V X K V E S V Y G N
O U A E O U F Q J X S Q F N T
F K V I M A L B X B P A B U V
K N Z V O X P W Z B C Z J D J
I W S H W V O T S E I C E P S
P N H O H E K I A D D G Y O N
```

Fun Fact

So far, scientists have classified more than a million different animals. Would you believe that about 95% of all the animals in the world are invertebrates? That's a lot of animals without backbones! Most of these invertebrates are arthropods. Insects, spiders, and crabs are arthropods.

Classifying Animals

Vertebrates are animals with backbones. There are five classes of vertebrates: fish, amphibians, birds, reptiles, and mammals. List five vertebrates that live in your house or neighborhood. Write which class of vertebrate each of the animals belongs to.

1. _____cat_____ _____mammal_____

2. _____ _____

3. _____ _____

4. _____ _____

5. _____ _____

Name _____

The semantic map shows the main concept of this chapter in the center circle. The words by the outer circles are related to the main concept. Choose the phrase from the list that is related to each word. Write the phrase in the circle below the word.

how plants make food
knoblike structure in center of flower
when a cell and an egg combine
makes plants green

stalks that surround pistils
resting
small leaves below flowers
contains egg cells

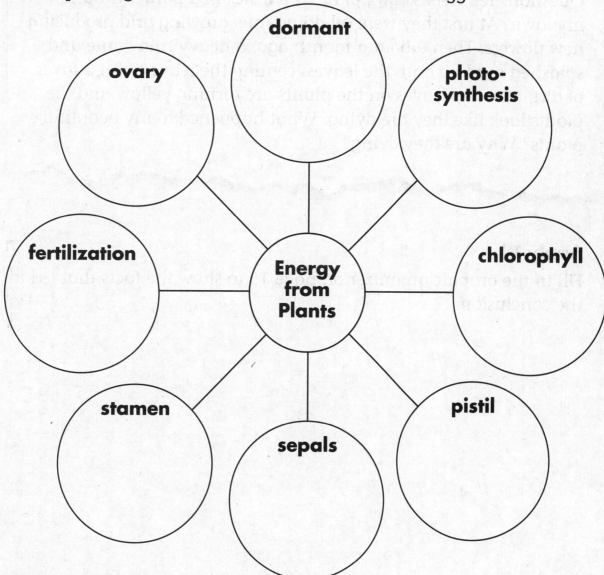

 Notes for Home: Your child learned the vocabulary terms for Chapter 2.
Home Activity: Have your child use illustrations from his or her textbook to provide examples that help define the vocabulary words. Use the words as you talk about how plants make their own food and reproduce.

Draw Conclusions

The Plant Doctor, Doctor Phil O. Dendron, received this letter from a reader. Read the reader's question and identify the facts and details that can help you draw a conclusion about why the plants died.

Ask the Plant Doctor

Question: Ten weeks ago I planted pansies in a border around my lawn. At first they were all doing fine, growing and producing new flowers. Then, about a month ago, a heavy rain came and splashed mud up onto the leaves, coating the leaves with a layer of dirt. Now the leaves on the plants are turning yellow and the plants look like they are dying. What happened to my beautiful plants? Why are they dying?

Apply It!

Fill in the graphic organizer on page 15 to show the facts that led to the conclusion.

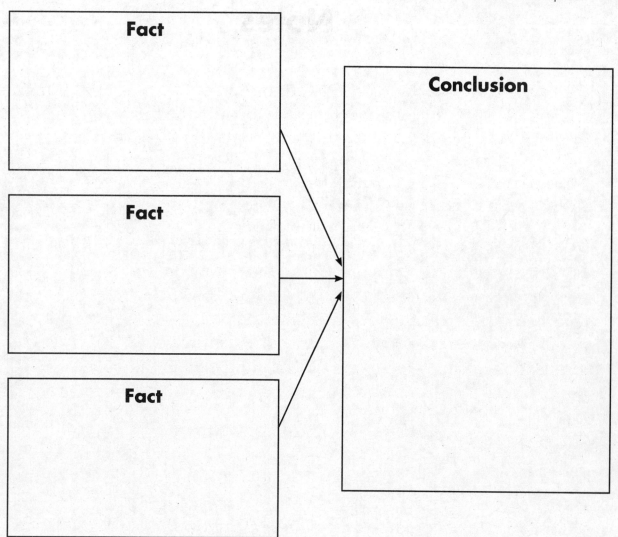

Fact

Fact

Fact

Conclusion

Notes for Home: Your child practiced the skill of drawing conclusions. He or she used the skill to determine why plants were dying.

Home Activity: Make up a scenario in which a pet is missing. Provide facts and details that will allow your child to draw conclusions about where the pet has gone.

Notes

Name _____

Lesson 1: What are plants' characteristics?

Before You Read Lesson 1

Read each statement below. Place a check mark in the circle to indicate whether you agree or disagree with the statement.

		Agree	Disagree
1.	Plants produce their own food.	○	○
2.	Water and soil are all that a plant needs to survive.	○	○
3.	Plants are green because they contain chlorophyll.	○	○
4.	Water can enter a plant through its leaves and through its roots.	○	○

After You Read Lesson 1

Reread each statement above. If the lesson supports your choice, place a check mark in the *Correct* circle. Then explain how the text supports your choice. If the lesson does not support your choice, place a check mark in the *Incorrect* circle. Then explain why your choice is wrong.

		Correct	Incorrect
1.	_____	○	○
	_____		
2.	_____	○	○
	_____		
3.	_____	○	○
	_____		
4.	_____	○	○
	_____		

Notes for Home: Your child has completed a pre/post inventory of key concepts in the lesson.
Home Activity: Have your child describe to you how plants use photosynthesis to produce their own food.

Reviewing Terms: Sentence Completion

Complete each sentence with the correct word or phrase.

_____ 1. The process by which plants make sugar is called _____. (photosynthesis, stoma)

_____ 2. _____ is the substance in plants that captures the Sun's energy. (Chlorophyll, Carbon dioxide)

Reviewing Concepts: Sentence Completion

Complete each sentence with the correct word or phrase.

_____ 3. Plants are made up of _____. (one cell, many cells)

_____ 4. Plants need carbon dioxide and _____ to carry out photosynthesis. (water, sugar)

_____ 5. The roots, stems, and leaves of plants store extra _____. (sugar, oxygen)

_____ 6. Stomas are found on the underside of _____. (roots, leaves)

_____ 7. Chlorophyll makes plants _____. (green, tall)

_____ 8. Sugar and oxygen are the _____ of photosynthesis. (starting materials, products)

Applying Strategies: Converting Units

9. Redwood trees can grow to be 90 meters tall. How many centimeters are equal to 90 meters? Show your work. (2 points) Hint: 1 meter = 100 centimeters.

© Pearson Education, Inc.

Lesson 2: What are the parts of plants?

Before You Read Lesson 2

Read each statement below. Place a check mark in the circle to indicate whether you agree or disagree with the statement.

		Agree	Disagree
1.	All plants have leaves, stems, and roots.	○	○
2.	The stem of a plant carries water, minerals, and food between the roots and the leaves.	○	○
3.	The roots of a plant make and store food.	○	○
4.	A carrot is a root that contains stored food.	○	○

After You Read Lesson 2

Reread each statement above. If the lesson supports your choice, place a check mark in the *Correct* circle. Then explain how the text supports your choice. If the lesson does not support your choice, place a check mark in the *Incorrect* circle. Then explain why your choice is wrong.

		Correct	Incorrect
1.	_____ _____	○	○
2.	_____ _____	○	○
3.	_____ _____	○	○
4.	_____ _____	○	○

Notes for Home: Your child has completed a pre/post inventory of key concepts in the lesson.
Home Activity: Have your child name and describe the functions of the parts of a plant found in your home or yard.

Reviewing Concepts: True or False

Write **T** (True) or **F** (False) on the line before each statement.

_____ 1. The role of plant leaves is to produce food for the plant.

_____ 2. A tree trunk is a kind of stem.

_____ 3. All plant stems carry out photosynthesis.

_____ 4. A plant's roots make food for the plant.

_____ 5. The individual roots in a fibrous root system are all about the same size.

_____ 6. Fibrous roots grow very deep in the soil.

_____ 7. Most grasses have taproots.

_____ 8. Taproots store food for the plant.

Applying Strategies: Draw Conclusions

Use complete sentences to answer question 9. (2 points)

9. A plant has large, flat leaves. What conclusion can you draw about the amount of water that is usually available in this plant's habitat?

_____

_____

_____

Lesson 3: How do plants reproduce?

Before You Read Lesson 3

Read each statement below. Place a check mark in the circle to indicate whether you agree or disagree with the statement.

		Agree	Disagree
1.	All plants make new plants in the same way.	○	○
2.	Plants have male and female structures that combine to make seeds.	○	○
3.	Most flowers have four main parts.	○	○
4.	All plants are pollinated by insects.	○	○

After You Read Lesson 3

Reread each statement above. If the lesson supports your choice, place a check mark in the *Correct* circle. Then explain how the text supports your choice. If the lesson does not support your choice, place a check mark in the *Incorrect* circle. Then explain why your choice is wrong.

		Correct	Incorrect
1.	_____	○	○
	_____		
2.	_____	○	○
	_____		
3.	_____	○	○
	_____		
4.	_____	○	○
	_____		

 Notes for Home: Your child has completed a pre/post inventory of key concepts in the lesson.
Home Activity: Have your child summarize the role of pollen in the reproduction of plants.

Reviewing Terms: Matching

Match each description with the correct word. Write the letter on the line next to each description.

_____ 1. small green leaves below a flower's petals

_____ 2. the female organ of the plant; part that produces egg cells

_____ 3. the male part of the plant

_____ 4. the thick bottom part of the pistil

_____ 5. the process of egg and sperm combining

a. ovary

b. sepals

c. fertilization

d. pistil

e. stamen

Reviewing Concepts: True or False

Write **T** (True) or **F** (False) on the line before each statement.

_____ 6. One way to classify plants is by how they reproduce.

_____ 7. Most flowers have four main parts.

_____ 8. After fertilization, seeds develop in a plant's sepal.

Writing

Use a complete sentence to answer question 9. (2 points)

9. Write a sentence that describes the role of colorful, sweet-smelling flowers in plant reproduction.

_____

_____

Name _____

Lesson 4: What is the life cycle of a plant?

Before You Read Lesson 4

Read each statement below. Place a check mark in the circle to indicate whether you agree or disagree with the statement.

		Agree	Disagree
1.	Seeds need warm temperatures to grow.	○	○
2.	All plants grow from seeds.	○	○
3.	A good place to plant a seed is underneath the plant it came from.	○	○
4.	The life cycle of some plants can be as long as 4,000 years.	○	○

After You Read Lesson 4

Reread each statement above. If the lesson supports your choice, place a check mark in the *Correct* circle. Then explain how the text supports your choice. If the lesson does not support your choice, place a check mark in the *Incorrect* circle. Then explain why your choice is wrong.

		Correct	Incorrect
1.	_____	○	○
	_____		
2.	_____	○	○
	_____		
3.	_____	○	○
	_____		
4.	_____	○	○
	_____		

Notes for Home: Your child has completed a pre/post inventory of key concepts in the lesson.
Home Activity: Have your child compare the life cycle of a plant to the life cycle of an animal.

© Pearson Education, Inc.

Name _____

Reviewing Terms: Sentence Completion

Complete the sentence with the correct word.

_____ 1. A seed stays _____ if it does not have the right conditions to germinate. (dormant, growing)

Reviewing Concepts: Sentence Completion

Complete each sentence with the correct word.

_____ 2. When conditions are right, a seed _____. (germinates, pollinates)

_____ 3. Fruits with tiny hooks are most likely spread by _____. (wind, animals)

_____ 4. Most seeds that plants make _____ grow to be new plants. (do, never)

_____ 5. A spore must land on _____ ground to germinate. (wet, dry)

_____ 6. Mosses have a _____ step life cycle. (one, two)

_____ 7. A bulb is an underground _____. (stem, flower)

_____ 8. Cuttings can be taken from a plant's stem, roots, or _____. (flowers, leaves)

Applying Strategies: Compare and Contrast

Use complete sentences to answer question 9. (2 points)

9. Describe one similarity and one difference between spores and seeds.

_____

_____

_____

_____

Workbook

How Sunlight Affects Fruit Production

Tomato plants and snow pea plants both need sunlight to produce fruit. But a good gardener knows not to plant these plants in the same spot in the garden. That is because they each have different sunlight needs. Four tomato plants and four snow pea plants were planted in different areas of a garden. Each area received different amounts of sunlight. The numbers of tomatoes and snow peas harvested from each plant at the first picking were measured. The graph shows the results.

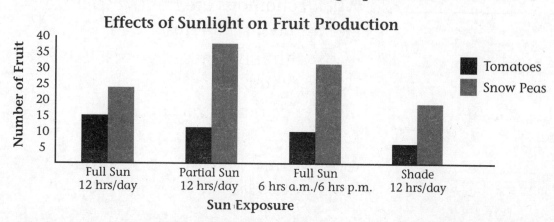

Effects of Sunlight on Fruit Production

Use the graph to answer the questions. Circle the letter of the answer.

1. What kind of sun exposure produces the most tomatoes?
   A. Full Sun for 12 hours a day
   B. Partial Sun for 12 hours a day
   C. 6 hours of full Sun in the morning and in the evening
   D. Shade for 12 hours a day

2. Which statement best summarizes the information in the graph?
   A. Both tomato plants and snow pea plants produce best when they receive full Sun all day.
   B. Both tomato plants and snow pea plants produce best when they receive some shade.
   C. Tomato plants produce best in the shade, and snow peas produce best with full Sun exposure.
   D. Tomato plants produce best when they receive full Sun all day, and snow peas produce best when they receive partial Sun all day.

Notes for Home: Your child learned how to read a double bar graph. He or she used the bar graph to examine the effects of sunlight on fruit production in plants.
Home Activity: Have your child ask you questions that you can answer by reading the bar graph.

Notes

Take Home Booklet

Use with Chapter 2

Dear Family,

Your child is learning how plants make their own food and reproduce. In the science chapter Energy from Plants, our class has learned about plant parts and their functions. We have focused on how plants use energy to make food. Students have also learned the varied ways plants reproduce.

In addition to learning how plants make their own food, students have also learned many new vocabulary words. Help your child to make these words a part of his or her own vocabulary by using them when you talk together about plants.

> chlorophyll
> dormant
> fertilization
> photosynthesis
> pistil
> sepal
> stamen
> ovary

These following pages include activities that you and your child can do together. By participating in your child's education, you will help to bring the learning home.

Family Science Activity
Exploring Plant Growth: Seeds' Needs

Materials:

- 2 wet seeds (pinto seeds work well)
- 2 clear glasses
- Paper towels
- 1 sheet of black construction paper
- Scissors
- Tape

Steps

1. Tape the black construction paper around one of the glasses. Save a small square of the paper to cover the glass with later.
2. Wet the paper towels. Fill half of each glass with paper towels.
3. Place a seed in each glass. The seeds should lie within the paper towel.
4. Set the small square of black construction paper on the top of the covered glass.
5. Place both glasses on a sunny windowsill. Keep the paper towels in both glasses moist.
6. Encourage your child to observe the seeds in each glass over several days. Have your child describe each seed's growth.
7. Talk about why the seed in the covered glass had little or no growth compared to the seed in the uncovered glass.

Workbook

Plant Parts

Unscramble the words below. Each word names a part of a flower. An example has been done for you.

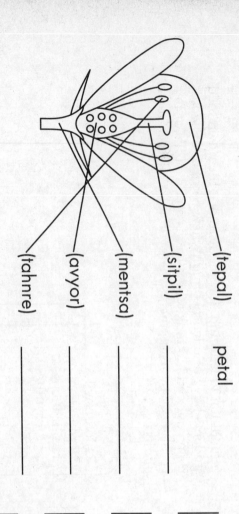

(tepal)   petal

(sitpil)   _____

(mentsa)   _____

(avyor)   _____

(tahnre)   _____

Plant Reproduction

Look at the plants below. Write an S if the plant grows from a seed, a B if it grows from a bulb, or an R if it grows from a runner. An example has been done for you.

 S

 _____

 _____

 _____

 _____

_____

Fun Fact

A Venus's Flytrap is a plant. It grows from a bulb. The soil it lives in has few nutrients. To survive, a Venus's Flytrap must catch and eat insects! How? There are small hairs on the plant's leaves. When an insect causes the hairs to move, the leaves snap shut. About a week later, the leaves open. Only the insects' exoskeleton is left behind.

Name _____

Use the hints to match each vocabulary word with its definition.
Draw a line from the word box to the definition box.

carnivores (Hint: In Spanish, *carne* means "meat.")	Organisms that break down dead plant and animal tissues
community (Hint: You belong to a community.)	Organisms that eat only plants
decomposers (Hint: *Decompose* means "to break down.")	All the living and nonliving things in an environment and the way they interact
ecosystem (Hint: A lake, a pond, and a forest are all ecosystems.)	All the members of one species that live within an area of an ecosystem
herbivores (Hint: Herbs are plants.)	Formed by the different populations that interact with each other in the same area
niche (Hint: A person who has found the perfect job has found his or her "niche.")	Organisms that eat only animals
omnivores (Hint: The prefix *omni-* means "all" or "every.")	The specific role an organism has in its habitat
population (Hint: All the students in your school make up the student population.)	Organisms that eat both plants and animals

Notes for Home: Your child learned the vocabulary terms for Chapter 3.
Home Activity: Read a nature book with your child. Have your child use the vocabulary words to describe the characteristics and habitats of the plants and animals you read about.

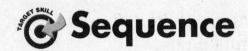

Sequence

Read the science article.

Energy in Ecosystems

Sunlight is the main source of energy in any ecosystem. **First,** plants use the Sun's energy, air, soil, and water to make their own food. They are producers. **Then** animals eat, or consume, the plants. They are consumers. **Next,** these animals are eaten by other animals called carnivores. Finally, the plants and animals die, and decomposers, such as insects, eat the remains. Decomposers break down the dead plant and animal tissues into minerals and nutrients that are put back into the soil, air, and water.

Apply It!

Fill in the graphic organizer on the next page to show the flow of energy through an ecosystem.

Name _____

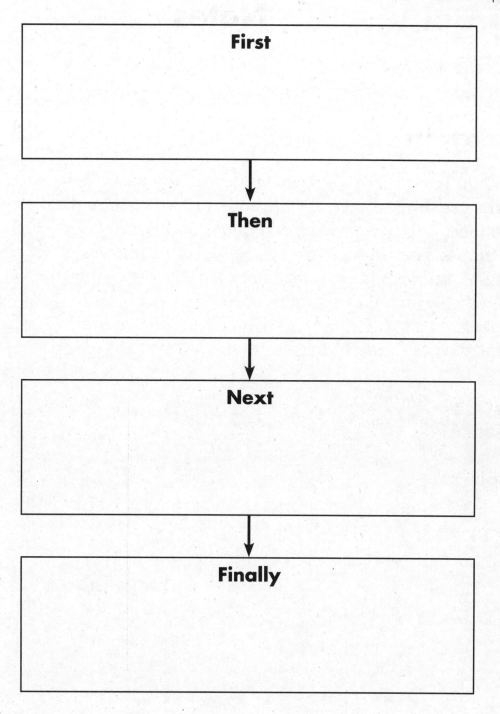

First

Then

Next

Finally

Notes for Home: Your child learned how to sequence a series of events.
Home Activity: Have your child tell about the main events in his or her typical day using the words *first, then, next,* and *finally.*

Notes

Name _____

Lesson 1: What are the parts of ecosystems?

Before You Read Lesson 1

Read each statement below. Place a check mark in the circle to indicate whether you agree or disagree with the statement.

	Agree	Disagree
1. A river is part of an ecosystem.	○	○
2. A community is a group of similar organisms.	○	○
3. Some plants and animals have adaptations that help them survive in the desert.	○	○
4. Animals sharing the same habitat have similar niches.	○	○

After You Read Lesson 1

Reread each statement above. If the lesson supports your choice, place a check mark in the *Correct* circle. Then explain how the text supports your choice. If the lesson does not support your choice, place a check mark in the *Incorrect* circle. Then explain why your choice is wrong.

	Correct	Incorrect
1. _____ _____	○	○
2. _____ _____	○	○
3. _____ _____	○	○
4. _____ _____	○	○

Notes for Home: Your child has completed a pre/post inventory of key concepts in the lesson.
Home Activity: Have your child compare and contrast a desert ecosystem and a tropical rain forest ecosystem.

© Pearson Education, Inc.

Name _____

Reviewing Terms: Sentence Completion

Complete each sentence with the correct word.

Ecosystem **1.** A(n) _____ is all the living and nonliving things in an environment. (ecosystem, niche)

Community **2.** All of the members of one species that live in an area of an ecosystem are a _____. (population, habitat)

Habitats **3.** A _____ is the different populations that interact in an area. (niche, community)

population **4.** An organism's _____ is its role in its habitat. (adaptation, niche)

Reviewing Concepts: True or False

Write **T** (True) or **F** (False) on the line before each statement.

_T_ **5.** Air, water, soil, and sunlight are nonliving parts of ecosystems.

_T_ **6.** Deserts are the driest kind of ecosystem.

_F_ **7.** A tundra ecosystem is always warm.

_T_ **8.** Rainforest ecosystems get rain all through the year.

Applying Strategies: Calculating

9. In a forest ecosystem, the number of individual birds in a population is counted each year. If there were 2,927 birds in Year 1, and 1,958 birds in Year 2, by how many birds did the population decrease? Show your work. (2 points)

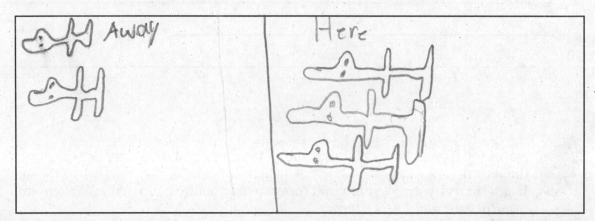

Lesson 2: How does energy flow in ecosystems?

Before You Read Lesson 2

Read each statement below. Place a check mark in the circle to indicate whether you agree or disagree with the statement.

	Agree	Disagree
1. Only living parts of an ecosystem are affected by the energy from the Sun.	O	O
2. In an ecosystem, insects help put minerals and nutrients back into the soil.	O	O
3. Plants are the first link in any food chain.	O	O
4. When the rain forests are cut down, it affects the food web of the ecosystem.	O	O

After You Read Lesson 2

Reread each statement above. If the lesson supports your choice, place a check mark in the *Correct* circle. Then explain how the text supports your choice. If the lesson does not support your choice, place a check mark in the *Incorrect* circle. Then explain why your choice is wrong.

	Correct	Incorrect
1. _____ _____	O	O
2. _____ _____	O	O
3. _____ _____	O	O
4. _____ _____	O	O

Notes for Home: Your child has completed a pre/post inventory of key concepts in the lesson.
Home Activity: Have your child draw an illustration to help explain how a food chain works.

Reviewing Terms: Matching

Match each description with the correct word. Write the letter on the line next to each description.

_____ 1. consumers that eat only plants   **a.** omnivores

_____ 2. consumers that eat only animals   **b.** herbivores

_____ 3. consumers that eat plants and animals   **c.** decomposers

_____ 4. consumers that digest waste and   **d.** carnivores
          remains of dead plants and animals

Reviewing Concepts: Sentence Completion

Complete each sentence with the correct word or phrase.

_____ 5. A(n) _____ might eat some of the same foods as a carnivore. (herbivore, omnivore)

_____ 6. An animal with sharp claws and teeth is most likely a(n) _____. (herbivore, carnivore)

_____ 7. In a food chain, energy flows in _____. (two directions, one direction)

_____ 8. Food chains all start with energy from _____. (sunlight, consumers)

Applying Strategies: Sequence

9. The sentences below tell how decomposers affect ecosystems, but the sentences are out of order. Use the clue words to write the sentences in the correct order. (2 points)

Finally, animals eat the plants.
Next, minerals and nutrients are put back in the soil.
First, decomposers digest waste and the remains of dead organisms.
Then living plants use the materials.

_____

_____

_____

_____

© Pearson Education, Inc.

Lesson 3: How does matter flow in ecosystems?

Before You Read Lesson 3

Read each statement below. Place a check mark in the circle to indicate whether you agree or disagree with the statement.

	Agree	Disagree
1. About one-half of Earth's surface is covered with water.	○	○
2. Organisms that carry out photosynthesis are producers.	○	○
3. Organisms decay quicker when they receive a lot of sunlight.	○	○
4. A coral reef is an example of an ecosystem.	○	○

After You Read Lesson 3

Reread each statement above. If the lesson supports your choice, place a check mark in the *Correct* circle. Then explain how the text supports your choice. If the lesson does not support your choice, place a check mark in the *Incorrect* circle. Then explain why your choice is wrong.

	Correct	Incorrect
1. _____ _____	○	○
2. _____ _____	○	○
3. _____ _____	○	○
4. _____ _____	○	○

Notes for Home: Your child has completed a pre/post inventory of key concepts in the lesson.
Home Activity: Have your child compare how matter flows through an ecosystem with the way in which energy flows through an ecosystem.

Reviewing Concepts: True or False

Write **T** (True) or **F** (False) on the line before each statement.

_____ 1. The same animals live in freshwater and saltwater habitats.

_____ 2. Algae are producers in water ecosystems.

_____ 3. A food web shows how food chains are connected.

_____ 4. Decay always happens at the same rate in ecosystems.

_____ 5. Decay happens faster when there is more moisture.

_____ 6. Fungi and bacteria are two kinds of decomposers.

_____ 7. The process of decay releases carbon dioxide into the atmosphere.

_____ 8. The colder the temperature, the faster decay happens.

Writing

Use complete sentences to answer question 9. (2 points)

9. Write a description of what would happen if there were no decomposers in an ecosystem.

_____

_____

_____

_____

Graphing Water Temperature

Scientists wanted to find out about the effects of water temperature on the fish population in a local river. First they gathered data about the temperature of the water over time. Here is the line graph they made using that data.

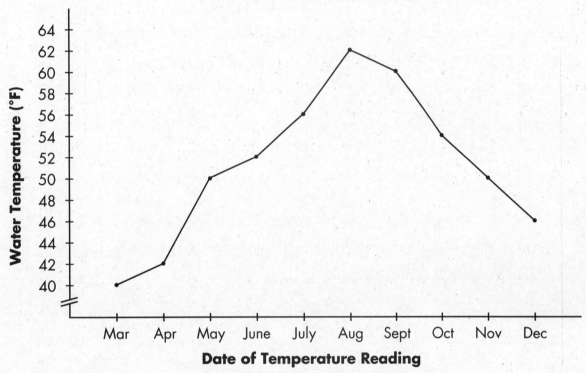

Change in Water Temperature

Use the graph to answer these questions.

1. In which month was the water temperature the highest?
   - A. March
   - B. June
   - C. August
   - D. September

2. What was the temperature of the water in April?
   - A. 32°F
   - B. 42°F
   - C. 50°F
   - D. 62°F

3. In which two months was the temperature the same?
   - A. March and April
   - B. April and December
   - C. July and August
   - D. May and November

Notes for Home: Your child learned how to read a line graph.
Home Activity: Look for line graphs on the weather page or another page of a newspaper. Together with your child interpret the information displayed on the graphs.

Notes

Dear Family,

Your child is learning the ways and places in which different organisms live. In the science chapter Ecosystems, our class has learned how plants and animals interact with each other and with their environments. Students have also learned how living things get their energy and how that energy flows through an ecosystem.

In addition to learning about the living and nonliving parts of an ecosystem, students have also learned many new vocabulary words. Help your child to make these words a part of his or her own vocabulary by using them when you talk together about ecosystems.

ecosystem
population
community
niche
herbivores
carnivores
omnivores
decomposers

The following pages include activities that you and your child can do together. By participating in your child's education, you will help to bring the learning home.

© Pearson Education, Inc.

Family Science Activity

Make a Collage of Living Things

Help your child remember how living things are classified by making a colorful collage of different plants and animals.

Materials

- Magazines
- Scissors
- Glue
- Pens, pencils, or markers
- Cardboard or construction paper

Steps

1. Use magazines to find pictures of different plants and animals. Try to find many examples of mammals, birds, reptiles, amphibians, fish, and different invertebrates.
2. Cut out the pictures and glue them onto the cardboard or construction paper.
3. Label each picture. You can use the Internet or an encyclopedia to help you.

Talk About It

How many plants are in the collage?
How many different types of animals are in the collage?
How many mammals are in the collage? reptiles? birds? invertebrates?
Why are cats, bears, monkeys, and humans all considered mammals?

Workbook

Unscramble the letters to find the vocabulary words.
Use the circled letters to answer the riddle below.

V O I C S E R R A N | __ | __ | __ | __ | __ | __ | __ | __ | __ | (○)10 | __

N P A L T U O P I O | __ | __ | __ | __ | __ | __ | __ | __ | __ | (○)10 | __

R S D O E S P M O C E | __ | __ | __ | __ | __ | __ | (○)11 | __ | __ | __ | __

S T E Y E M C O S | __ | __ | __ | __ | __ | (○)6 | __ | __ | __

M N R O O I E S V | (○)1 | __ | __ | __ | __ | __ | __ | (○)9 | __

M Y U C I N T M O | __ | (○)2 | __ | (○)4 | __ | __ | __ | __ | __

E N H C I | __ | __ | __ | (○)8 | __

S B E V E R H O R I | __ | __ | (○)3 | __ | (○)5 | __ | (○)7 | __ | __ | __

The natural places where people, animals, and
plants live is called an

(○)1 (○)2 (○)3 (○)4 (○)5 (○)6 (○)7 (○)8 (○)9 (○)10 (○)11

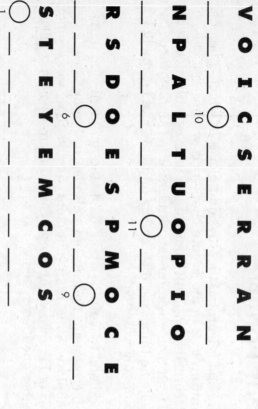

Fun Fact

Mammals come in all shapes and sizes. The
smallest living mammal is the bumblebee bat.
It weighs about two grams—even lighter than
a penny! The largest living mammal is the blue
whale. It can get as long as 100 feet and weigh
as much as 150 tons!

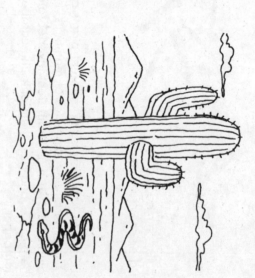

Answers: CARNIVORES, POPULATION, DECOMPOSERS, ECOSYSTEM, OMNIVORES,
COMMUNITY, NICHE, HERBIVORES, ENVIRONMENT

Choose the word from the list on the left that completes
each sentence on the right. Write the letter of the word on
the line.

Word List	Sentence
a competition	____ 1. Dinosaurs are species that are now ____.
b parasite	____ 2. Poisonous and disease-causing trash is called ____.
c host	____ 3. Wolves and coyotes are in ____ for the resources in their ecosystem.
d succession	____ 4. A rose plant can be a ____ for insects such as aphids.
e hazardous waste	____ 5. Species that are in danger of becoming extinct are called ____ species.
f extinct	____ 6. ____ is still occurring in the environment that was disturbed when Mt. St. Helens erupted in 1980.
g endangered	____ 7. A flea on a dog is a ____.

Notes for Home: Your child learned the vocabulary terms for Chapter 4.
Home Activity: Have your child use each of the words in a sentence.

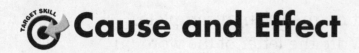
⊙ Cause and Effect

> # Mt. St. Helens
>
> In 1980, Mt. St. Helens, a volcano in Washington, erupted. The eruption damaged about 500 square kilometers of forest. The mountain exploded and rocks and gases poured out of it. The very high temperatures (about 600° C) of the rocks and gases resulted in the deaths of all organisms just north of the crater. It was a huge eruption. For 25 kilometers around the volcano, trees were knocked down, torn from the ground, and crashed down the mountain. Very few plants survived the avalanche and great heat. Some, however, did not have their roots torn from the ground. They resprouted and grew again.

Apply It!

Use the graphic organizer on page 35 to show what happened around Mt. St. Helens and why it happened.

Cause

Effect

1. Mount St. Helens erupted in 1980.

1. _____
_____
_____
_____

2. _____
_____
_____

2. All organisms just north of the crater died.

3. The eruption was huge.

3. _____
_____
_____
_____

4. _____
_____
_____
_____

4. Plants resprouted and grew again.

Notes for Home: Your child learned how to identify cause and effect.
Home Activity: Read an article in the newspaper with your child and help him or her identify cause-and-effect relationships in the article.

Notes

Lesson 1: How are ecosystems balanced?

Before You Read Lesson 1

Read each statement below. Place a check mark in the circle to indicate whether you agree or disagree with the statement.

	Agree	Disagree
1. A desert is a good environment for a cow.	○	○
2. Proper balance between populations is necessary for a healthy ecosystem.	○	○
3. Changes cause an unbalanced ecosystem.	○	○

After You Read Lesson 1

Reread each statement above. If the lesson supports your choice, place a check mark in the *Correct* circle. Then explain how the text supports your choice. If the lesson does not support your choice, place a check mark in the *Incorrect* circle. Then explain why your choice is wrong.

	Correct	Incorrect
1. _____	○	○
_____		
2. _____	○	○
_____		
3. _____	○	○
_____		

Notes for Home: Your child has completed a pre/post inventory of key concepts in the lesson.
Home Activity: Discuss with your child the amount of resources required to sustain a large city compared to the amount needed to sustain a small town.

Reviewing Concepts: True or False

Write **T** (True) or **F** (False) on the line before each statement.

_____ 1. Plants and animals need food, water, space, shelter, light, and air to grow.

_____ 2. Living things can only survive in environments where their needs are met.

_____ 3. All of the parts of an ecosystem are interrelated.

_____ 4. Animals provide the oxygen that plants need to live.

_____ 5. Every kind of living thing needs the same kind of soil and weather.

_____ 6. When an ecosystem is balanced, none of its parts are changing.

_____ 7. Water that evaporates from an ecosystem is replaced when it rains or snows.

_____ 8. All organisms help keep the balance of an ecosystem.

Applying Strategies: Cause and Effect

Use complete sentences to answer question 9. (2 points)

9. A cause is shown here. Use complete sentences to describe two possible effects.

   Cause: The number of a certain kind of animal in an ecosystem increases.

   Effect: _____

   Effect: _____

Name _____

Lesson 2: How do organisms interact?

Before You Read Lesson 2

Read each statement below. Place a check mark in the circle to indicate whether you agree or disagree with the statement.

	Agree	Disagree
1. Only members of the same species compete for resources within their ecosystem.	○	○
2. Some animals reduce competition by feeding at different times of day.	○	○
3. Insects that feed on a plant and harm it are called hosts.	○	○

After You Read Lesson 2

Reread each statement above. If the lesson supports your choice, place a check mark in the *Correct* circle. Then explain how the text supports your choice. If the lesson does not support your choice, place a check mark in the *Incorrect* circle. Then explain why your choice is wrong.

	Correct	Incorrect
1. _____	○	○
_____		
2. _____	○	○
_____		
3. _____	○	○
_____		

Notes for Home: Your child has completed a pre/post inventory of key concepts in the lesson.
Home Activity: Discuss how living things in the natural environment around your home share and compete for resources.

Reviewing Terms: Matching

Match each description with the correct word. Write the letter on the line next to each description.

_____ 1. when two or more species need the
same resources

_____ 2. the organism that is helped in a close
relationship between two living things

_____ 3. the organism that is harmed in a close
relationship between two living things

a. host

b. competition

c. parasite

Reviewing Concepts: Sentence Completion

Complete each sentence with the correct word.

_____ 4. Populations _____ when all of their needs are
met. (increase, decrease)

_____ 5. An organism that competes successfully is
_____ likely to reproduce. (more, less)

_____ 6. Competition is _____ when two kinds
of animals hunt at different times of day.
(increased, decreased)

_____ 7. Lichens are fungi and _____ that live together.
(algae, mosses)

_____ 8. Parasites _____ the organism they live on.
(help, harm)

Writing

Use complete sentences to answer question 9. (2 points)

9. Write two sentences that describe ways living in a group helps
animals to survive.

_____

_____

_____

Lesson 3: How do environments change?

Before You Read Lesson 3

Read each statement below. Place a check mark in the circle to indicate whether you agree or disagree with the statement.

		Agree	Disagree
1.	Environments continually experience many changes.	○	○
2.	Changes in climate affect the kinds of organisms that live in an ecosystem.	○	○
3.	Fossils tell us little about past environments.	○	○

After You Read Lesson 3

Reread each statement above. If the lesson supports your choice, place a check mark in the *Correct* circle. Then explain how the text supports your choice. If the lesson does not support your choice, place a check mark in the *Incorrect* circle. Then explain why your choice is wrong.

		Correct	Incorrect
1.	_____	○	○
	_____		
2.	_____	○	○
	_____		
3.	_____	○	○
	_____		

Notes for Home: Your child has completed a pre/post inventory of key concepts in the lesson.
Home Activity: Help your child name animals that are now extinct or endangered, such as the homing pigeon, dinosaurs, grey bat, key deer, and blue whale.

Reviewing Terms: Matching

Match each description with the correct word. Write the letter on the line next to each description.

_____ 1. a gradual change in an ecosystem   **a.** succession

_____ 2. a species that has completely died out   **b.** endangered

_____ 3. a species that is reduced and may   **c.** extinct
die out

Reviewing Concepts: Sentence Completion

Complete each sentence with the correct word or phrase.

_____ 4. Succession typically occurs _____. (all at once, in stages)

_____ 5. Climates change very _____. (slowly, quickly)

_____ 6. In modern times, _____ are the main reason animals become extinct. (meteors, human activities)

_____ 7. Fossils show that Earth has _____ over time. (changed, stayed the same)

_____ 8. Fossils show that woolly mammoths are very similar to today's _____. (elephants, giraffes)

Applying Strategies: Compare and Contrast

Use complete sentences to answer question 9. (2 points)

9. Name one similarity and one difference between extinct and endangered species.

_____

_____

_____

_____

_____

Name _____

Lesson 4: How do people disturb the balance?

Before You Read Lesson 4

Read each statement below. Place a check mark in the circle to indicate whether you agree or disagree with the statement.

	Agree	Disagree
1. All organisms change their environment to meet their needs.	○	○
2. Wastes and chemicals pollute water.	○	○
3. Strip-mining is an environmentally friendly way to get coal from Earth.	○	○

After You Read Lesson 4

Reread each statement above. If the lesson supports your choice, place a check mark in the *Correct* circle. Then explain how the text supports your choice. If the lesson does not support your choice, place a check mark in the *Incorrect* circle. Then explain why your choice is wrong.

	Correct	Incorrect
1. _____	○	○
2. _____	○	○
3. _____	○	○

Notes for Home: Your child has completed a pre/post inventory of key concepts in the lesson.
Home Activity: Discuss with your child sources of water pollution and things individuals can do to help reduce it.

© Pearson Education, Inc.

Reviewing Terms: Sentence Completion

Complete the sentence with the correct word or phrase.

_____ 1. A substance that is very harmful to humans and other living things is _____. (reclaimed, hazardous waste)

Reviewing Concepts: True or False

Write **T** (True) or **F** (False) on the line before each statement.

_____ 2. When humans change the environment, the balance of ecosystems is never changed.

_____ 3. Lichens are good indicators of air quality.

_____ 4. Pollutants in rivers and streams can move into Earth's oceans.

_____ 5. Oil spills are not harmful to animals.

_____ 6. Strip mining does not harm the ecosystems nearby.

_____ 7. Today, land that is mined is reclaimed.

_____ 8. The National Parks System preserves the habitats of many animals.

Applying Strategies: Calculating

9. Each person throws away about two kilograms of garbage each day. How many kilograms of garbage would five people throw away in two days? Show your work. (2 points)

Frogs and Fractions

In 1990, toxic waste polluted a wetlands area. Later scientists saw that many frogs in the wetlands were born with deformed feet. The scientists worked for 10 years to clean up the wetlands. Over the years, they studied the frog population to see what fraction of the frogs had deformed feet. The circle graphs below show their findings.

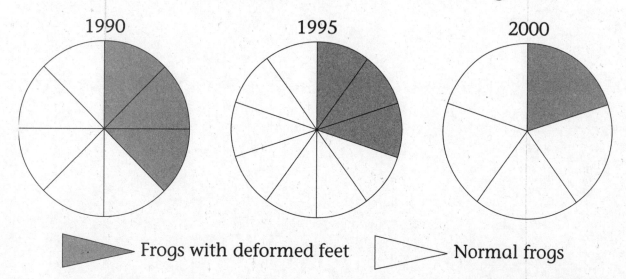

1990   1995   2000

◣——— Frogs with deformed feet   ◁——— Normal frogs

Use the graphs above to answer the questions.

1. In 1990, what fraction of the frogs had deformed feet?
   A. $\frac{1}{5}$
   B. $\frac{3}{8}$
   C. $\frac{1}{3}$
   D. $\frac{5}{8}$

2. In 1995, what fraction of the frogs had normal feet?
   A. $\frac{7}{3}$
   B. $\frac{3}{7}$
   C. $\frac{7}{10}$
   D. $\frac{3}{10}$

3. In 2000, what fraction of the frogs had deformed feet?
   A. $\frac{1}{5}$
   B. $\frac{1}{4}$
   C. $\frac{4}{5}$
   D. $\frac{5}{4}$

4. In 2000, what fraction of the frogs had normal feet?
   A. $\frac{1}{5}$
   B. $\frac{4}{5}$
   C. $\frac{1}{4}$
   D. $\frac{5}{4}$

Notes for Home: Your child learned how to identify a fraction of circle graphs.
Home Activity: Make groups of two objects, such as pens and pencils or pennies and dimes, and have your child use fractions to identify the parts of the group.

Notes

Dear Family,

Your child is learning how living things interact in an ecosystem. In the science chapter Changes in Ecosystems, our class has learned how living things depend on each other. Students have also learned how changes to the environment affect living things.

In addition to learning about the how ecosystems are balanced, students have also learned many new vocabulary words. Help your child to make these words a part of his or her own vocabulary by using them when you talk together about living things and their environments.

competition
parasite
host
succession
extinct
endangered
hazardous waste

The following pages include activities that you and your child can do together. By participating in your child's education, you will help to bring the learning home.

Family Science Activity
A Local Ecosystem

In this activity, you will help your child understand that living things interact with one another and with nonliving things to meet their needs. You will do this by examining a plot of ground to see what it contains.

Materials:

- Meter sticks or rulers
- Garden trowels
- Aluminum or plastic trays
- Hand lenses
- Toothpicks
- Gloves
- Paper and pens or pencils

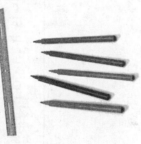

Steps

1. Discuss what different ecosystems contain.
2. Go outside and measure a plot of ground that is 1 square meter.
3. Predict the kinds of living and nonliving things you will find in the ground. Write your predictions on the paper.
4. Use a garden trowel to take a small sample of soil from the ground and spread it on a tray.
5. Use a hand lens and toothpick to examine the soil for living and nonliving things. Add your observations to the paper.
6. Return the soil to the ground.
7. Discuss the living and nonliving things that you found in the soil. How do they form an ecosystem? How do they interact?

Workbook

Vocabulary Practice

Fill in the blanks with the correct vocabulary word.

1. _____ are substances that are very harmful to humans and other organisms.

2. A _____ is an organism that lives on or in another organism.

3. Living things are in _____ when they must use the same limited resources.

4. Organisms that are in danger of becoming extinct are called _____.

5. The passenger pigeon is _____. Its entire species has died and is gone forever.

Fun Fact

The bald eagle is the national symbol of America. In 1782, there may have been more than 250,000 bald eagles in the continental United States. But, by 1963, the bald eagle was an endangered species. Less than 1,000 bald eagles were alive due to hunting and the destruction of their habitats. Today, laws and regulations have helped the bald eagle population to recover. There are now more than 20,000 bald eagles in 48 states.

Answers: 1. hazardous wastes, 2. parasite, 3. competition, 4. endangered species, 5. extinct

Literacy and Art
Competing Animals

When two or more populations share an ecosystem, there may be competition for some of the same resources. Draw a picture of a wild animal in the box below. Tell about its habitat. What does it need to survive? What other animals is it in competition with?

Each sentence gives a clue about the vocabulary term that completes the sentence. The vocabulary term also appears in scrambled form in parentheses after the sentence. Use clues and the scrambled words to complete the sentences.

1. Kicking a ball is controlled by _____. (nvlauoryt seusmcl)

2. Breathing is controlled by _____. (nvlairuonyt csumsle)

3. A _____ carries information in the form of electrical signals. (renonu)

4. _____ are organisms that cause disease. (gohneaspt)

5. You can pass an _____ to someone else. (siunofietc edsiase)

6. Your _____ helps protect you from getting infections. (einmum mseyts)

7. A _____ makes you immune to a disease. (evnaicc)

Notes for Home: Your child learned the vocabulary terms for Chapter 5.
Home Activity: Ask your child how these pairs of vocabulary terms are related: *voluntary muscles/involuntary muscles, pathogens/infectious disease, immune system/ vaccine.*

Draw Conclusions

Read the science article.

Blood Cholesterol

High blood cholesterol is one of the major causes of heart disease. Cholesterol is a fat-like substance in blood. It builds up in arteries and can block the flow of blood to the heart. Blood carries oxygen to the heart. If blood and oxygen are blocked from getting to the heart, the result can be a heart attack.

Lowering cholesterol levels helps reduce the chances of having a heart attack. Eating foods that are low in saturated fats, such as non-fat dairy products, lean meat, skinless poultry, whole grains, fruits, and vegetables, can lower cholesterol levels.

Name _____

Apply It!

Write facts from the article in the graphic organizer.
Then use these facts to draw a conclusion. Write your
conclusion in the graphic organizer.

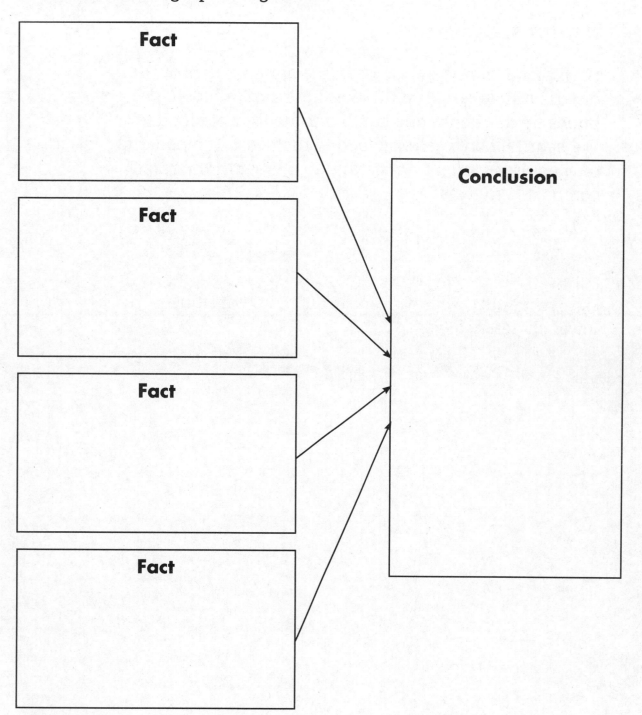

Fact

Fact

Fact

Fact

Conclusion

Notes for Home: Your child learned how to draw conclusions based on facts.
Home Activity: Discuss how physical activity contributes to a person's health.
Have your child draw conclusions about the benefits of regular exercise.

Notes

Lesson 1: What are the skeletal and muscular systems?

Before You Read Lesson 1

Read each statement below. Place a check mark in the circle to indicate whether you agree or disagree with the statement.

	Agree	Disagree
1. Your heart is part of your skeletal system.	O	O
2. Your skeleton is made of tissue.	O	O
3. Bones store calcium and produce blood cells.	O	O
4. We can control all the muscles in our body.	O	O

After You Read Lesson 1

Reread each statement above. If the lesson supports your choice, place a check mark in the *Correct* circle. Then explain how the text supports your choice. If the lesson does not support your choice, place a check mark in the *Incorrect* circle. Then explain why your choice is wrong.

	Correct	Incorrect
1. _____	O	O
_____		
2. _____	O	O
_____		
3. _____	O	O
_____		
4. _____	O	O
_____		

Notes for Home: Your child has completed a pre/post inventory of key concepts in the lesson.
Home Activity: Have your child summarize how our skeleton and muscles are used for support and movement.

Reviewing Terms: Matching

Match each description with the correct phrase. Write the letter on the line next to each description.

_____ 1. muscles you control

_____ 2. muscles you cannot control

a. involuntary muscles

b. voluntary muscles

Reviewing Concepts: Sentence Completion

Complete each sentence with the correct word or phrase.

_____ 3. Similar cells that work together form _____. (tissues, organs)

_____ 4. The human heart is one example of a(n) _____. (tissue, organ)

_____ 5. Bones are tissues that make up the _____ system. (skeletal, muscular)

_____ 6. Bones store _____ for the body. (minerals, energy)

_____ 7. Skeletal muscles work _____. (alone, in pairs)

_____ 8. Cardiac muscles and smooth muscles are both _____ muscles. (voluntary, involuntary)

Applying Strategies: Compare and Contrast

Use a complete sentence to answer question 9. (2 points)

9. Write a sentence that describes a way to build strong bones.

_____

_____

Name _____

Lesson 2: What are the respiratory and circulatory systems?

Before You Read Lesson 2

Read each statement below. Place a check mark in the circle to indicate whether you agree or disagree with the statement.

	Agree	Disagree
1. Your body needs carbon dioxide to use the nutrients in the food you eat.	○	○
2. Our respiratory system helps us breathe.	○	○
3. Your mouth is part of your respiratory system.	○	○
4. Veins carry oxygen-rich blood to the body.	○	○

After You Read Lesson 2

Reread each statement above. If the lesson supports your choice, place a check mark in the *Correct* circle. Then explain how the text supports your choice. If the lesson does not support your choice, place a check mark in the *Incorrect* circle. Then explain why your choice is wrong.

	Correct	Incorrect
1. _____	○	○
_____		
2. _____	○	○
_____		
3. _____	○	○
_____		
4. _____	○	○
_____		

Notes for Home: Your child has completed a pre/post inventory of key concepts in the lesson.
Home Activity: Use illustrations in your child's text to help him or her explain how our respiratory and circulatory systems work.

Reviewing Concepts: Matching

Match each body part in the left column with the correct system in the right column. Write the letter of the correct answer on the line. You will use each answer more than once.

_____ 1. lungs

_____ 2. heart

_____ 3. diaphragm

_____ 4. bronchial tube

_____ 5. blood vessels

_____ 6. trachea

_____ 7. blood

_____ 8. air sacs

a. respiratory system

b. circulatory system

Applying Strategies: Draw Conclusions

Use complete sentences to answer question 9. (2 points)

9. List two facts that support the conclusion below.

   Conclusion: The respiratory and circulatory systems work together to bring oxygen to the cells of the body.

   Fact: _____

   _____

   Fact: _____

   _____

Name _____

Lesson 3: What are the digestive and nervous systems?

Before You Read Lesson 3

Read each statement below. Place a check mark in the circle to indicate whether you agree or disagree with the statement.

	Agree	Disagree
1. Digestion begins in your mouth.	○	○
2. Most digestion takes place in your stomach.	○	○
3. Coughing is controlled by your spinal cord.	○	○
4. Your eyes tell your nervous system how to respond to information they receive.	○	○

After You Read Lesson 3

Reread each statement above. If the lesson supports your choice, place a check mark in the *Correct* circle. Then explain how the text supports your choice. If the lesson does not support your choice, place a check mark in the *Incorrect* circle. Then explain why your choice is wrong.

	Correct	Incorrect
1. _____ _____	○	○
2. _____ _____	○	○
3. _____ _____	○	○
4. _____ _____	○	○

 Notes for Home: Your child has completed a pre/post inventory of key concepts in the lesson.
Home Activity: Have your child draw a picture of the parts of the digestive system and use the illustration to explain how the digestive system works.

Reviewing Terms: Sentence Completion

Complete the sentence with the correct word or phrase.

_____ 1. The basic unit of the nervous system is the _____.
(neuron, spinal cord)

Reviewing Concepts: True or False

Write **T** (True) or **F** (False) on the line before each statement.

_____ 2. Digestion begins in the stomach.

_____ 3. Nutrients pass into the blood in the lungs.

_____ 4. The circulatory system carries nutrients to the cells
in the body.

_____ 5. The esophagus is a tube that connects the mouth
to the stomach.

_____ 6. The central nervous system is made up of your bones
and spinal cord.

_____ 7. Reflexes are quick, automatic responses.

_____ 8. The skull helps protect the brain from injury.

Applying Strategies: Converting Units

9. The small intestine is about seven meters long. About how many
centimeters long is the small intestine? Show your work. (2 points)
Hint: 1 meter = 100 centimeters.

Name _____

Think, Read, Learn

Use with pages 156–161.

Lesson 4: How does the body defend itself?

Before You Read Lesson 4

Read each statement below. Place a check mark in the circle to indicate whether you agree or disagree with the statement.

	Agree	Disagree
1. Microorganisms fight infection.	○	○
2. Your skin is part of your defense system.	○	○
3. An infectious disease can be passed to someone else.	○	○
4. Pathogens are tiny organisms that live in your body and help fight disease.	○	○

After You Read Lesson 4

Reread each statement above. If the lesson supports your choice, place a check mark in the *Correct* circle. Then explain how the text supports your choice. If the lesson does not support your choice, place a check mark in the *Incorrect* circle. Then explain why your choice is wrong.

	Correct	Incorrect
1. _____	○	○
_____		
2. _____	○	○
_____		
3. _____	○	○
_____		
4. _____	○	○
_____		

 Notes for Home: Your child has completed a pre/post inventory of key concepts in the lesson.
Home Activity: Discuss with your child things you can do such as washing your hands, eating properly, and not sharing food, to keep from catching infectious diseases.

© Pearson Education, Inc.

Workbook

Reviewing Terms: Matching

Match each description with the correct word or phrase. Write the letter on the line next to each description.

_____ 1. organisms that cause some diseases

_____ 2. a disease that can pass from one organism to another

_____ 3. a body system that protects you from pathogens

_____ 4. a medicine that protects you from disease

a. vaccine

b. immune system

c. infectious disease

d. pathogens

Reviewing Concepts: Sentence Completion

Complete each sentence with the correct word or phrase.

_____ 5. Most disease-causing organisms are very _____. (large, small)

_____ 6. Your _____ is your body's first defense against pathogens. (skin, immune system)

_____ 7. Viruses and bacteria are two kinds of _____. (antibodies, pathogens)

_____ 8. A vaccine signals your body to make _____. (pathogens, antibodies)

Writing

Use complete sentences to answer question 9. (2 points)

9. Write two sentences. Each sentence should describe one historical development that has changed the way people fight disease.

_____

_____

_____

Units of Measure and the Human Body

Scientists usually use metric measurements to measure quantities. Liquids are measured in liters. Length is measured in meters. Speed is measured in number of meters traveled in a given time interval, such as 10 meters *per second.*

Choose and write the most appropriate unit to complete each sentence.

1. The average adult body contains about 4–5 _____
    of blood.

    milliliters   kiloliters

    liters   kilograms

2. Nerve signals in your brain travel between nerve cells at speeds of

    more than 100 _____.

    meters per minute   meters per second

    meters per hour   meters per day

3. The small intestine in the human body is about

    _____ in length.

    6 millimeters   6 meters

    6 centimeters   6 kilometers

4. Your esophagus is about 250 _____ long.

    kilometers   centimeters

    meters   millimeters

Notes for Home: Your child learned about metric measurements relating to the human body.
Home Activity: Find items around your home that are labeled in metric units, such as milk, dry goods, or medicine. Discuss the different units of measure with your child.

Notes

Dear Family,

Your child is learning about the human body. In the science chapter Systems of the Human Body, our class has learned how organs work as organ systems to carry out life processes. Students have also learned how the human body defends itself against disease.

In addition to learning about the how their bodies work, students have also learned many new vocabulary words. Help your child to make these words a part of his or her own vocabulary by using them when you talk together about the human body.

> voluntary muscles
> involuntary muscles
> neuron
> pathogens
> infectious disease
> immune system
> vaccine

The following pages include activities that you and your child can do together. By participating in your child's education, you will help to bring the learning home.

Family Science Activity

Plastic Bottle Lungs

Help your child understand the respiratory system. Talk about how air enters and leaves the lungs when we inhale and exhale. The model described below should help demonstrate this concept.

Materials:

- 1-liter plastic bottle
- Two large balloons
- Two rubber bands
- Scissors
- Paper
- Pens or pencils

Steps

1. Cut the plastic bottle in half horizontally. Keep the top half of the bottle. Discard the lower half.
2. Place one of the balloons through the opening of the bottle.
3. Stretch the balloon opening over the bottle opening.
4. Place a rubber band over this balloon to keep it in place.
5. Cut the neck off the other balloon. Stretch this balloon across the bottom of the bottle.
6. Use the other rubber band to hold the second balloon in place.
7. Explain that the balloon in the opening of the bottle represents the lungs. The balloon across the bottom of the bottle represents the diaphragm.
8. Pull down on the bottom balloon and then let go. Try pulling slowly. Pull quickly. What happens to the balloon in the bottle opening? Record all observations. How is this like breathing?

Workbook

Connecting to Content

So Many Systems!

The human body is a complex machine made of many systems. Decide the job of each system listed below.

organ system
skeletal system
muscular system
respiratory system
circulatory system
digestive system
nervous system
immune system

1. Your body would not be able to walk, throw, smile, or sing without your _____.

2. Your _____ helps your body when you are feeling sick.

3. A group of organs that work together make up an _____.

4. Your _____ carries signals from your brain to the rest of your body.

5. Your _____ supports and protects your body. It is made mostly of bone.

6. Your heart is the most important organ in your _____.

7. Your _____ helps you to get energy from the food you eat.

8. The system that controls your breathing is called the _____.

Workbook

Each vocabulary word is used in a sentence. Write the letter of the correct definition on the line in front of the sentence.

Definition	Word		Definition
_____	1. **evaporation**: On a sunny day, **evaporation** causes puddles to dry up.	**a**	scientist who studies weather conditions
_____	2. **condensation**: The dew on the grass is **condensation**.	**b**	any form of water that falls to Earth
_____	3. **precipitation**: Snow and rain are **precipitation**.	**c**	amount of water vapor in the air
_____	4. **barometer**: The **barometer** is showing an increase in air pressure.	**d**	a tool used to measure air pressure
_____	5. **anemometer**: The pilot read the **anemometer** to check wind strength.	**e**	the changing of water to water vapor
_____	6. **wind vane**: The **wind vane** was pointing to the north.	**f**	the area where two air masses meet
_____	7. **humidity**: The air is very wet and sticky when the **humidity** is high.	**g**	a device that shows the direction from which the wind is blowing
_____	8. **front**: A cold **front** is moving in, so we can expect rain.	**h**	the changing of water vapor to liquid water
_____	9. **meteorologist**: The **meteorologist** predicted the storm.	**i**	a tool used to measure wind speed

Notes for Home: Your child learned the vocabulary terms for Chapter 6.
Home Activity: Listen to or read a weather report with your child to see how many of the vocabulary words are used in the report.

 Cause and Effect

Read the newspaper article.

Global Warming

The increase in Earth's average temperature is called global warming. Scientists say that the greenhouse effect is one cause of global warming. Earth heats up as gases in the atmosphere trap energy from the Sun. People produce some of these gases. They use cars and electricity. The fuels burned to run cars and produce electricity emit gases into the air.

Global warming can lead to changes in Earth's climate. In turn, these changes may affect ecosystems. They may result in higher sea levels. They might cause droughts. This could reduce the amount of food that farmers can grow. This could lead to famine.

Apply It!

Use the graphic organizer on page 55. Write a cause for each effect given. Write an effect for each cause given.

Effect	**Cause**
1. global warming	1. _____ _____ _____
2. _____ _____ _____	2. Gases in the atmosphere trap energy from the Sun.
3. _____ _____ _____	3. People use cars and electricity.
4. Seas might rise.	4. _____ _____ _____
5. Amount of crops grown is reduced.	5. _____ _____ _____

Notes for Home: Your child learned how to identify causes and effects of global warming.
Home Activity: Look at causes and results of activities at home. Name a cause and have your child name effects.

Notes

Lesson 1: Where is Earth's water?

Before You Read Lesson 1

Read each statement below. Place a check mark in the circle to indicate whether you agree or disagree with the statement.

	Agree	Disagree
1. Most of Earth's water is in rivers and lakes.	○	○
2. The salt in the ocean comes from the rocks and soil on land.	○	○
3. All ocean water has the same amount of salt in it.	○	○

After You Read Lesson 1

Reread each statement above. If the lesson supports your choice, place a check mark in the *Correct* circle. Then explain how the text supports your choice. If the lesson does not support your choice, place a check mark in the *Incorrect* circle. Then explain why your choice is wrong.

	Correct	Incorrect
1. _____	○	○
_____		
2. _____	○	○
_____		
3. _____	○	○
_____		

Notes for Home: Your child has completed a pre/post inventory of key concepts in the lesson.
Home Activity: Look at a world, country, or state map to locate bodies of water. Discuss the source and drainage area of major rivers.

Reviewing Concepts: True or False

Write **T** (True) or **F** (False) on the line before each statement.

_____ 1. Earth's water can exist as a solid, a liquid, or a gas.

_____ 2. More of Earth's surface is land than is water.

_____ 3. Very few organisms live in water.

_____ 4. The ocean's saltiness is the same in all locations.

_____ 5. The salt in the ocean comes from rocks and soils on land.

_____ 6. The warmer the ocean water, the more salt can dissolve in it.

_____ 7. Most of Earth's water is fresh water.

_____ 8. All of Earth's water can be used for people to drink.

Applying Strategies: Using Decimals

9. More than $\frac{97}{100}$ of Earth's water is in oceans and seas. Less than $\frac{1}{100}$ is in rivers and lakes. Write decimals that are equivalent to these two fractions. (2 points)

$$\frac{97}{100} =$$
$$\frac{1}{100} =$$

Lesson 2: How do water and air affect weather?

Before You Read Lesson 2

Read each statement below. Place a check mark in the circle to indicate whether you agree or disagree with the statement.

	Agree	Disagree
1. The Earth's water cycle ends when fresh water drains into the oceans.	○	○
2. Clouds are formed by condensation.	○	○
3. Air pressure is higher at higher elevations.	○	○

After You Read Lesson 2

Reread each statement above. If the lesson supports your choice, place a check mark in the *Correct* circle. Then explain how the text supports your choice. If the lesson does not support your choice, place a check mark in the *Incorrect* circle. Then explain why your choice is wrong.

	Correct	Incorrect
1. _____ _____	○	○
2. _____ _____	○	○
3. _____ _____	○	○

Notes for Home: Your child has completed a pre/post inventory of key concepts in the lesson.
Home Activity: Look at the national weather report in the newspaper. Compare the weather in areas near the ocean to the weather in inland areas.

Name _____

Reviewing Terms: Matching

Match each description with the correct word. Write the letter on the line next to each description.

_____ 1. the process of liquid water changing to water vapor

_____ 2. the process of water vapor changing to liquid water

_____ 3. any form of water that falls to Earth

a. precipitation

b. condensation

c. evaporation

Reviewing Concepts: Sentence Completion

Complete each sentence with the correct word or phrase.

_____ 4. The higher the temperature, the _____ water changes to a gas. (faster, slower)

_____ 5. The water cycle is powered by energy from _____. (the Sun, gravity)

_____ 6. The total amount of water on Earth _____ changes. (slowly, never)

_____ 7. Most of Earth's atmosphere is _____. (nitrogen, oxygen)

_____ 8. The pushing force of air is called _____. (gravity, air pressure)

Applying Strategies: Cause and Effect

Use a complete sentence to answer question 9. (2 points)

9. Write a sentence that describes the effect of air becoming cool and dense.

_____

_____

Lesson 3: What are air masses?

Before You Read Lesson 3

Read each statement below. Place a check mark in the circle to indicate whether you agree or disagree with the statement.

	Agree	Disagree
1. Air masses can be warm or cold.	○	○
2. Cold fronts can cause thunderstorms.	○	○
3. When the water vapor in clouds gets too warm, the vapor turns into liquid water.	○	○

After You Read Lesson 3

Reread each statement above. If the lesson supports your choice, place a check mark in the *Correct* circle. Then explain how the text supports your choice. If the lesson does not support your choice, place a check mark in the *Incorrect* circle. Then explain why your choice is wrong.

	Correct	Incorrect
1. _____	○	○
_____		
2. _____	○	○
_____		
3. _____	○	○
_____		

Notes for Home: Your child has completed a pre/post inventory of key concepts in the lesson.
Home Activity: Look at clouds or pictures of clouds. Ask your child to describe the clouds.

Name _____

Use with pages 190–193.

Reviewing Terms: Sentence Completion

Complete the sentence with the correct word or phrase.

_____ 1. _____ is the amount of water vapor in the air.
(Humidity, Air mass)

_____ 2. A _____ is a place where two air masses meet.
(cloud, front)

Reviewing Concepts: True or False

Write **T** (True) or **F** (False) on the line before each statement.

_____ 3. The movement of air masses can be used to predict weather.

_____ 4. Global winds usually blow from east to west.

_____ 5. Air masses mix at fronts.

_____ 6. Cold air has a higher density than warm air.

_____ 7. Warm fronts move more quickly than cold fronts.

_____ 8. Clouds are classified by their size, color, and shape.

Applying Strategies: Compare and Contrast

Use complete sentences to answer question 9. (2 points)

9. How are air masses that form over land different from air masses that form over water? How are they similar?

_____

_____

_____

_____

_____

© Pearson Education, Inc.

58A Lesson Review

Workbook

Lesson 4: How do we measure and predict weather?

Before You Read Lesson 4

Read each statement below. Place a check mark in the circle to indicate whether you agree or disagree with the statement.

	Agree	Disagree
1. Ocean currents affect the weather worldwide.	○	○
2. Air pressure can only be measured with scientific tools.	○	○
3. Earth's climate remains the same over time.	○	○

After You Read Lesson 4

Reread each statement above. If the lesson supports your choice, place a check mark in the *Correct* circle. Then explain how the text supports your choice. If the lesson does not support your choice, place a check mark in the *Incorrect* circle. Then explain why your choice is wrong.

	Correct	Incorrect
1. _____	○	○
_____		
2. _____	○	○
_____		
3. _____	○	○
_____		

Notes for Home: Your child has completed a pre/post inventory of key concepts in the lesson.
Home Activity: Read or listen to a weather forecast with your child. Help your child identify the different measurements that are reported.

Name _____

Reviewing Terms: Matching

Match each description with the correct word or phrase. Write the letter on the line next to each description.

_____ 1. a scientist that studies weather
_____ 2. a tool that measures air pressure
_____ 3. a tool that measures wind speed
_____ 4. a tool that shows wind direction

a. wind vane
b. barometer
c. anemometer
d. meteorologist

Reviewing Concepts: Sentence Completion

Complete each sentence with the correct word or phrase.

_____ 5. Water heats and cools more _____ than land. (slowly, quickly)

_____ 6. When air pressure is _____, the weather is usually sunny and bright. (low, high)

_____ 7. Meteorologists use a _____ to measure the amount of rainfall. (hygrometer, rain gauge)

_____ 8. Triangles and half-circles are used on weather maps to show _____. (temperatures, fronts)

Writing

Use complete sentences to answer question 9. (2 points)

9. Describe two ways scientists can learn about Earth's past weather and climate.

_____

_____

_____

_____

_____

_____

Name _____

Reading Line Graphs

The line graph below shows how much the average temperature changes in California from month to month. Use the graph to answer the questions.

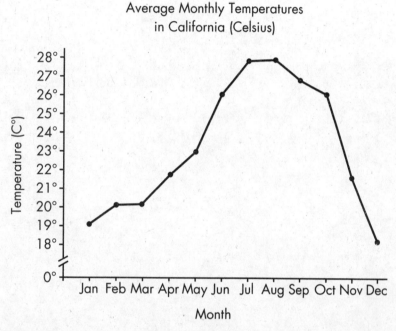

Average Monthly Temperatures in California (Celsius)

Use the line graph above to answer the questions.

1. What are the warmest months in California? How do you know?

    _____

    _____

2. What is the range of average temperatures?

    _____

3. Between which two consecutive months does the temperature increase the most? decrease the most?

    _____

4. Which months have the same average temperature?

    _____

    _____

Notes for Home: Your child learned how read a line graph.
Home Activity: Look through newspapers or magazines for line graphs. Discuss the information displayed in the graphs.

Notes

Dear Family,

Your child is learning what causes weather and how it can be predicted. In the science chapter Water Cycle and Weather, our class has learned how Earth's water affects the weather. Students have also learned the difference between freshwater and ocean water and how the water cycle contributes to our freshwater supply.

In addition to learning about the water cycle, the students have also learned many new vocabulary words. Help your child to make these words a part of his or her own vocabulary by using them when you talk together about weather.

evaporation
condensation
precipitation
humidity
front
meteorologist
barometer
anemometer
wind vane

The following pages include activities that you and your child can do together. By participating in your child's education, you will help to bring the learning home.

Family Science Activity
Build a Terrarium

Making and observing a terrarium can help your child understand how the water cycle works. Begin by discussing the stages of the water cycle: evaporation, precipitation, and condensation. Talk about what clouds are made of, why it rains, and where the water goes after it rains.

Materials:

- Clear plastic container with lid
- Soil
- Plant seeds (marigolds, herbs, and lima beans are reliable and grow fast)
- Water
- Large sunny window or grow light

Steps

1. Put an inch of soil in the bottom of the plastic container.
2. Plant a seed according to the package instructions. Add water.
3. Close the container. Place it next to a sunny window.
4. Have your child draw a picture of the terrarium and label it.
5. Encourage your child to predict what will happen to the plant if no additional water is added.
6. Have your child observe the terrarium daily. These observations can be recorded in writing or in pictures.
7. Over time, the lid of the terrarium will get misty. The plants will continue to grow without additional water being added. Discuss how the soil is still moist; the water evaporates, gets trapped by the lid, and condenses. Then, it "rains" in the terrarium.

Workbook

Vocabulary Practice

Unscramble the letters to find the vocabulary words. Then, use the circled letters to answer the riddle.

AICOTPIITNREP

– – – – – – – – – – (8) – – – –

MNATERMEOE

– – – – – (5) – – – –

FTRNO

– – (3) – –

IENRTOVAPAO

– (10) – – – (2) – – – –

VWDIANEN

(1) – – – – – –

RTITGEOOSEOLM

– – – – – (9) – – – –

TDOEONNICNSA

– (6) – – – – – – – –

MHTDUIIY

– – – (7) – – – –

EOAERTBMR

– – – (4) – – – – –

What is the name of the process that involves evaporation, condensation, and precipitation?

The ◯◯◯◯◯ ◯◯◯◯◯
  1 2 3 4 5   6 7 8 9 10

Connecting to Content

Which Weather Tool?

Meteorologists use many different tools and instruments to measure and predict the weather.

Draw a line to match the list of tools to their uses.

1. thermometer   measures air pressure

2. barometer   measures temperature

3. wind vane   measures the amount of rainfall

4. rain gauge   shows the direction from which the wind is blowing

Fun Fact

Most lakes contain fresh water. The Great Salt Lake in Utah is a saltwater lake. Its area covers about 1,700 square miles. Its water is saltier than ocean water. The world's largest saltwater lake is the Caspian Sea. It covers an area of 143,250 square miles.

Read each definition. Write the letter of each definition
next to the word it defines.

_____ 1. hurricane

a when the speed of storm winds increases
and winds begin to swirl

_____ 2. tropical
depression

b a rapidly spinning funnel of air that
descends from a thunderstorm cloud

_____ 3. tropical
storm

c when the winds of a tropical depression
begin to blow even faster and
thunderstorms move in spiral bands
toward the area of lowest air pressure

_____ 4. storm surge

d a dangerous storm with wind speeds of at
least 119 kilometers per hour

_____ 5. tornado

e a rise in sea level caused by a storm's
winds

_____ 6. vortex

f an area where air or liquid spins in circles

Notes for Home: Your child learned the vocabulary terms for Chapter 7.
Home Activity: Give your child a word. Have your child find an illustration in his
or her textbook that can be used to help define the term.

TARGET SKILL

Main Idea and Details

A Science Map

The map below shows areas with the greatest tornado activity in the United States.

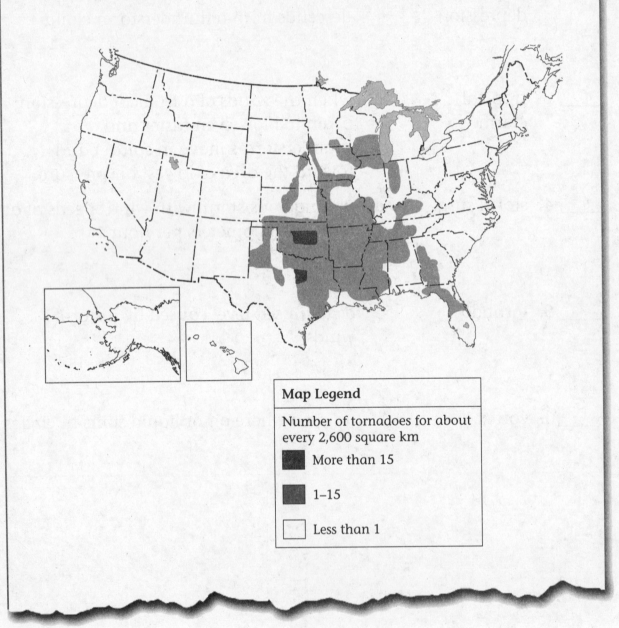

Map Legend

Number of tornadoes for about every 2,600 square km

More than 15

1–15

Less than 1

Apply It!

Use the graphic organizer below. List the main idea of the map on page 64. Then write in the details shown in the map.

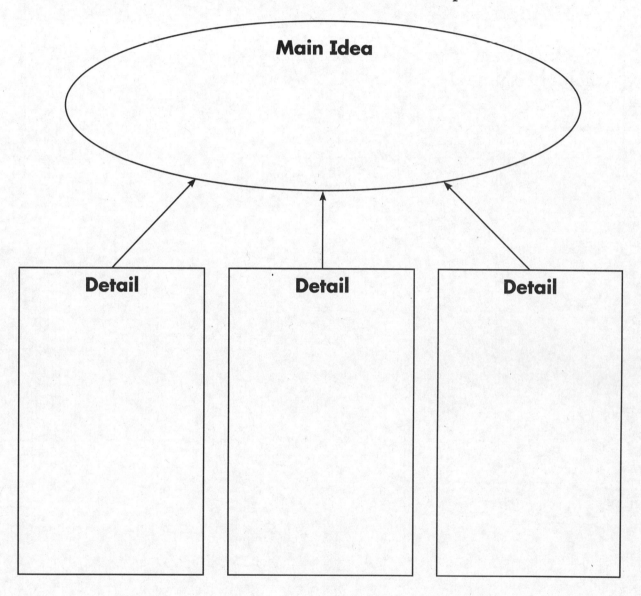

Notes for Home: Your child learned how to identify the main idea of a map.
Home Activity: Look for maps or pictures that illustrate a main idea. Have your child identify the main idea of each map or picture and details that support the main idea.

Notes

Name _____

Lesson 1: What are hurricanes?

Before You Read Lesson 1

Read each statement below. Place a check mark in the circle to indicate whether you agree or disagree with the statement.

	Agree	Disagree
1. Hurricanes reach speeds up to 500 kilometers per hour.	○	○
2. Thunderstorms can develop into tropical storms.	○	○
3. A hurricane gains energy as it moves closer to land.	○	○

After You Read Lesson 1

Reread each statement above. If the lesson supports your choice, place a check mark in the *Correct* circle. Then explain how the text supports your choice. If the lesson does not support your choice, place a check mark in the *Incorrect* circle. Then explain why your choice is wrong.

	Correct	Incorrect
1. _____	○	○
_____		
2. _____	○	○
_____		
3. _____	○	○
_____		

Notes for Home: Your child has completed a pre/post inventory of key concepts in the lesson.
Home Activity: Have your child describe hurricanes and the damage they can do. Have your child use the illustrations in the text to reinforce his or her description.

Name _____

Reviewing Terms: Matching

Match each description with the correct word or phrase. Write the letter on the line next to each description.

_____ 1. a dangerous storm with wind speeds of at least 119 km/hour

_____ 2. a storm with wind speeds up to 61 km/hour

_____ 3. a storm with wind speeds over 62 km/hour

_____ 4. the rise in sea level caused by a hurricane's winds

a. tropical storm

b. hurricane

c. tropical depression

d. storm surge

Reviewing Concepts: Sentence Completion

Complete each sentence with the correct word or phrase.

_____ 5. Hurricanes get their energy from warm _____. (ocean water, wind)

_____ 6. The _____ is found in the middle of the hurricane. (eye, storm surge)

_____ 7. Hurricanes are classified by their _____. (wind speed, rainfall amount)

_____ 8. A hurricane loses strength quickly over _____. (land, ocean water)

Applying Strategies: Main Idea and Details

Use complete sentences to answer question 9. (2 points)

9. Write two details that support the main idea shown below.

Main Idea: Tropical storms form only in certain conditions.

Detail: _____

_____

Detail: _____

_____

© Pearson Education, Inc.

Name _____

Lesson 2: What are tornadoes?

Before You Read Lesson 2

Read each statement below. Place a check mark in the circle to indicate whether you agree or disagree with the statement.

	Agree	Disagree
1. A tornado causes the air inside a thunderstorm to spin.	○	○
2. A vortex forms when a bathtub is drained.	○	○
3. A dust devil can develop into a tornado.	○	○

After You Read Lesson 2

Reread each statement above. If the lesson supports your choice, place a check mark in the *Correct* circle. Then explain how the text supports your choice. If the lesson does not support your choice, place a check mark in the *Incorrect* circle. Then explain why your choice is wrong.

	Correct	Incorrect
1. _____	○	○
_____		
2. _____	○	○
_____		
3. _____	○	○
_____		

© Pearson Education, Inc.

Notes for Home: Your child has completed a pre/post inventory of key concepts in the lesson.
Home Activity: Remind your child of the tornado in the classic movie *The Wizard of Oz*. Discuss what the tornado looked like and the damage it caused.

Reviewing Terms: Matching

Match each description with the correct word. Write the letter on the line next to each description.

_____ 1. a spinning column of air that touches the ground

_____ 2. an area where air or liquid spins in circles

a. tornado

b. vortex

Reviewing Concepts: True or False

Write **T** (True) or **F** (False) on the line before each statement.

_____ 3. Tornados form in strong thunderstorms.

_____ 4. Most tornados happen in autumn and winter.

_____ 5. A tornado can always be seen.

_____ 6. Doppler radar can be used to study tornados.

_____ 7. A tornado warning means that a tornado *might* form.

_____ 8. Hurricanes and tornados both spin around a center of low air pressure.

Writing

Use complete sentences to answer question 9. (2 points)

9. Write a list of three tips for tornado safety.

_____

_____

_____

_____

_____

Ranking Tornadoes

The Fujita Scale is used to measure a tornado's strength. Use the scale to answer the questions.

Rating	Type of Tornado	Estimated Wind Speeds in Kilometers per Hour
F0	Gale	64–116
Branches broken, chimneys damaged.		
F1	Moderate	117–180
Cars pushed off roads, shingles torn from roofs.		
F2	Significant	181–253
Roofs torn from some buildings, big trees torn from ground or split.		
F3	Severe	254–332
Walls and roofs torn from buildings, trees uprooted.		
F4	Devastating	333–419
Cars thrown, houses collapsed.		
F5	Incredible	420–512
Houses torn from foundations and collapsed, cars thrown more than 100 meters, concrete reinforced buildings damaged.		

1. Tornado winds are clocked at 415 kilometers per hour. What is the rating of this tornado?

   _____

2. A tornado tore roofs from buildings and split large trees. What is the rating of the tornado?

   _____

3. What type of damage might result from an F0 rated tornado?

   _____

 Notes for Home: Your child learned how to use the Fujita Scale to evaluate tornado damage.
Home Activity: Discuss safety procedures for storms. Talk about what the community and the family can do to reduce the risk during tornadoes.

Notes

Dear Family,

Your child is learning about hurricanes and tornadoes. In the science chapter Hurricanes and Tornadoes, our class has learned how hurricanes form, how scientists work together to predict hurricanes, and the impact hurricanes have on the environment. We have also learned how tornadoes form and why they are difficult for scientists to predict. Students have also learned how hurricanes and tornadoes are alike and different.

In addition to learning about tornadoes and hurricanes, the students have also learned many new vocabulary words. Help your child to make these words a part of his or her own vocabulary by using them when you talk together about severe weather.

> hurricane,
> tropical depression
> tropical storm
> storm surge
> tornado
> vortex

The following pages include activities that you and your child can do together. By participating in your child's education, you will help to bring the learning home.

Family Science Activity
Make a Model of a Tornado

Materials:

- Clear, wide-mouthed jar with lid
- Water
- Pepper or glitter

Steps

1. Fill the jar about two-thirds full of water.
2. Add about half of a tablespoon of pepper or glitter to the water.
3. Seal the jar with the lid.
4. Hold the top of the jar and slowly spin the jar in a circular movement. Encourage your child to describe the "tornado" that forms in the jar. Ask your child to identify the tornado's vortex.
5. Change the speed at which you spin the jar. Discuss how the shape of the tornado changes.

Workbook

Vocabulary Practice

Choose a vocabulary word to complete each riddle.

1. I form when winds increase and begin to swirl. My wind speeds reach up to 61 kilometers per hour.

I am a _____.

2. I am a dangerous tropical storm that forms near the Equator.

I am a _____.

3. I am a rise in sea level caused by a hurricane's winds.

I am a _____.

4. I form in strong thunderstorms. I have a column of spinning air that is shaped like a funnel.

I am a _____.

Connecting to Content

Name That Storm

Decide whether each characteristic below describes a tornado, hurricane, or both. Write a *T* for tornado. Write an *H* for hurricane. Write a *B* for both.

1. Has high winds _____

2. Forms over land _____

3. Can be hundreds of kilometers across _____

4. Can cause great damage _____

5. Most last only a few minutes _____

6. Forms over the ocean _____

Fun Fact

Hurricane names are chosen from six lists of names. Each name on the list starts with a different letter, starting with A. However, the letters Q, U, X, Y, and Z are not used. Names are taken off a list only after they are used to name a very destructive hurricane.

Each vocabulary term is used in a sentence to give you a clue about the term's meaning. Use the information to help you decide which term to write to complete each sentence in the box.

igneous rock: Many **igneous rocks** come to Earth's surface from volcanoes.

luster: A mineral's **luster** may be dull, metallic, pearly, glossy, greasy, or silky.

mineral: Most rocks are made of different combinations of **minerals**.

sediment: Lake bottoms are covered with layers of **sediment**.

sedimentary rock: **Sedimentary rocks** can be made from several different materials.

metamorphic rock: **Metamorphic rocks** can form from sedimentary rocks or from igneous rocks.

---

1. Rocks are made of _____, which are natural, nonliving solid crystals.

2. The way a mineral's surface reflects light is called its _____.

3. Eroded material found on the ocean floor is called _____.

4. Clay minerals cement layers of sediment together to form _____.

5. _____ is formed deep within Earth's crust.

6. Rock that has changed from one type of rock to another type of rock is called _____.

Notes for Home: Your child learned the vocabulary terms for Chapter 8.
Home Activity: Together look through your child's textbook, have your child find each vocabulary term, and read aloud the sentence in which the term appears.

 Summarize

Read the science article.

What Is a Mineral?

You down a glass of milk. It is rich with calcium. Is the calcium a mineral? According to mineralogists, scientists who study minerals, it is not. Why isn't the calcium a mineral? The calcium in milk is dissolved. It does not have a crystal structure. All minerals, according to mineralogists, have crystal structures. Therefore, for mineralogists, the calcium in milk is not a mineral.

Mineralogists use four features to distinguish minerals from other materials. (1) All minerals have a crystal structure. (2) Nature is the source of all minerals. Cubic zirconium looks like a mineral, but it is not one. It is made by people. (3) Each kind of mineral has its own chemical identity. Gold from California and gold from Africa are alike chemically. The makeup does not change because the gold came from different places. (4) Most minerals do not have any material that has ever been living.

Apply It!

You can use details in the article to help you summarize
the information. Use the graphic organizer. Record the
details. Then use the details to write a summary.

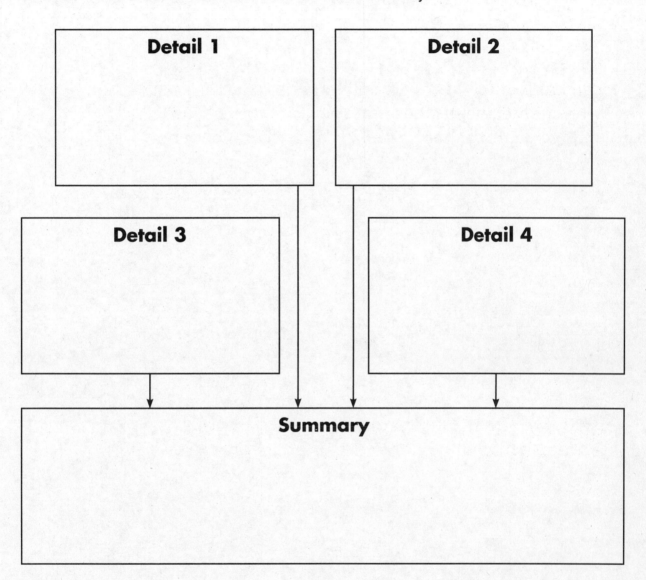

Detail 1

Detail 2

Detail 3

Detail 4

Summary

© Pearson Education, Inc.

Notes for Home: Your child learned to use details to summarize information.
Home Activity: Have your child find pictures of minerals in their text. Ask him or
her to tell why a mineralogist would say the picture shows a mineral.

Notes

Lesson 1: What are minerals?

Before You Read Lesson 1

Read each statement below. Place a check mark in the circle to indicate whether you agree or disagree with the statement.

		Agree	Disagree
1.	All types of granite are formed by the same combination of minerals.	○	○
2.	You can identify a mineral by its color alone.	○	○
3.	A diamond can scratch a piece of granite.	○	○
4.	The color of a mineral's streak depends on the color of the mineral.	○	○

After You Read Lesson 1

Reread each statement above. If the lesson supports your choice, place a check mark in the *Correct* circle. Then explain how the text supports your choice. If the lesson does not support your choice, place a check mark in the *Incorrect* circle. Then explain why your choice is wrong.

		Correct	Incorrect
1.	_____ _____	○	○
2.	_____ _____	○	○
3.	_____ _____	○	○
4.	_____ _____	○	○

Notes for Home: Your child has completed a pre-/post-inventory of key concepts in the lesson.
Home Activity: Collect some rocks from your yard or a nearby park. Discuss with your child the color, hardness, and streak of each.

Reviewing Terms: Matching

Match each description with the correct word. Write the letter on the line next to each description.

_____ 1. natural, nonliving solid crystals that make up rocks

_____ 2. the way a surface reflects light

a. luster

b. minerals

Reviewing Concepts: True or False

Write **T** (True) or **F** (False) on the line before each statement.

_____ 3. The crystals of all minerals have the same shape.

_____ 4. All rocks are made of minerals.

_____ 5. Physical properties are used to identify minerals.

_____ 6. The Mohs scale is used to rank a mineral's luster.

_____ 7. Color is one property of a mineral.

_____ 8. Streak is the color of powder a mineral leaves after being scratched on a special plate.

Applying Strategies: Decimals and Fractions

9. Pyrite can have a hardness of 6.5 on the Mohs scale. Write 6.5 as a mixed number. (2 points)

Lesson 2: How are sedimentary rocks formed?

Before You Read Lesson 2

Read each statement below. Place a check mark in the circle to indicate whether you agree or disagree with the statement.

		Agree	Disagree
1.	Plants break rocks into smaller pieces.	○	○
2.	Soil is a nonliving part of Earth's surface.	○	○
3.	Limestone forms from skeletons and shells.	○	○
4.	Fossils suggest that birds have been on Earth for more than 500 million years.	○	○

After You Read Lesson 2

Reread each statement above. If the lesson supports your choice, place a check mark in the *Correct* circle. Then explain how the text supports your choice. If the lesson does not support your choice, place a check mark in the *Incorrect* circle. Then explain why your choice is wrong.

		Correct	Incorrect
1.	_____ _____	○	○
2.	_____ _____	○	○
3.	_____ _____	○	○
4.	_____ _____	○	○

Notes for Home: Your child has completed a pre-/post-inventory of key concepts in the lesson.
Home Activity: Have your child summarize the ways in which different kinds of sedimentary rocks are formed.

Reviewing Terms: Matching

Match each description with the correct word or phrase. Write the letter on the line next to each description.

_____ 1. eroded material that settles at the bottom of lakes, rivers, and oceans

_____ 2. rock that forms when layers of particles cement together and harden

a. sediment

b. sedimentary rock

Reviewing Concepts: Sentence Completion

Complete each sentence with the correct word or phrase.

_____ 3. _____ is a sedimentary rock formed from materials that were once living. (Limestone, Sandstone)

_____ 4. _____ is the process that breaks down rocks. (Erosion, Weathering)

_____ 5. Fossils help scientists learn about Earth's _____. (future, past)

_____ 6. Fossils can help scientists determine the _____ of a rock layer. (age, size)

_____ 7. Newer layers of rock form _____ older layers. (above, below)

_____ 8. There are four major _____ in the geologic time scale. (time periods, rock types)

Writing

Use complete sentences to answer question 9. (2 points)

9. Describe how rocks are changed to soil.

_____

_____

_____

_____

Name _____

Lesson 3: What are igneous and metamorphic rocks?

Before You Read Lesson 3

Read each statement below. Place a check mark in the circle to indicate whether you agree or disagree with the statement.

	Agree	Disagree
1. Some rocks were once in a liquid state.	○	○
2. Once a rock is formed, it remains that type of rock forever.	○	○
3. Scientists must dig deep in Earth to find igneous rocks.	○	○
4. Only igneous rocks become metamorphic rocks.	○	○

After You Read Lesson 3

Reread each statement above. If the lesson supports your choice, place a check mark in the *Correct* circle. Then explain how the text supports your choice. If the lesson does not support your choice, place a check mark in the *Incorrect* circle. Then explain why your choice is wrong.

	Correct	Incorrect
1. _____	○	○
_____		
2. _____	○	○
_____		
3. _____	○	○
_____		
4. _____	○	○
_____		

 Notes for Home: Your child has completed a pre-/post-inventory of key concepts in the lesson.
Home Activity: Have your child explain the processes by which rocks change from one type of rock to another type of rock.

Name _____

Reviewing Terms: Matching

Match each description with the correct phrase. Write the letter on the line next to each description.

_____ 1. rocks that form when molten rock cools and hardens

_____ 2. rocks that have changed due to heat and pressure

a. metamorphic rocks

b. igneous rocks

Reviewing Concepts: True or False

Write **T** (True) or **F** (False) on the line before each statement.

_____ 3. Lava that cools above ground forms tiny crystals.

_____ 4. It can take more than a million years for magma to cool.

_____ 5. Metamorphic rocks are formed only from igneous rocks.

_____ 6. Slate is a metamorphic rock formed from shale.

_____ 7. The rock cycle is a process that is always occurring.

_____ 8. All rocks follow the same set of steps through the rock cycle.

Applying Strategies: Summarize

Use a complete sentence to answer question 9. (2 points)

9. Summarize how metamorphic rocks form.

_____

_____

_____

_____

Name _____

Large Numbers in Science

The table shows the age of Earth and the ages of fossils found around the world.

Fossil Record	Age in Years
Earth	4 billion, 600 million
Shark	360 million
Dinosaurs	225 million
Mushroom	90 million

Use the table to answer the questions. Circle the letter of the correct answer.

1. How old is Earth?
    A. 4,000,600,000   C. 4,600,000,000
    B. 4,006,000,000   D. 46,000,000,000

2. How old is the shark fossil?
    A. 360,000   C. 36,000,000
    B. 3,600,000   D. 360,000,000

3. How old are some dinosaur fossils?
    A. 225,000   C. 225,000,000
    B. 200,250,000   D. 2,250,000,000

4. How old is the mushroom fossil?
    A. 900,000   C. 9,000,000
    B. 90,000,000   D. 900,000,000

 Notes for Home: Your child learned how to read large numbers written in standard form.
Home Activity: Have your child subtract the numbers in the table to find the differences in age between any two of the fossils listed.

Notes

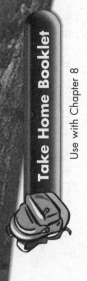

Dear Family,

Your child is learning what rocks are made of. In the science chapter Minerals and Rocks, our class has learned about the three types of rocks and how they form. Students have also learned how rocks can change from one form into another.

In addition to learning how rocks form and change, students have also learned many new vocabulary words. Help your child to make these words a part of his or her own vocabulary by using them when you talk together about rocks and minerals.

mineral
luster
sediment
sedimentary rock
igneous rock
metamorphic rock

The following pages include activities that you and your child can do together. By participating in your child's education, you will help to bring the learning home.

Family Science Activity
Growing Crystals

Materials:

- Glass jar
- Pencil
- Wool
- Warm water
- Salt
- Paper

Steps

1. Dissolve as much salt as possible into the jar of warm water. Continue to add salt and stir until the crystals stop dissolving.

2. Tie the wool around the pencil so that it rests in the saltwater. Leave the jar in a cool place.

3. As the water cools, salt crystals will grow on the wool. Each day, replace the water and add a fresh batch of dissolved salt.

4. Have your child record the growth and change of the crystals daily. Encourage him or her to draw the crystal formations.

5. After several days, look back at your child's observations. Discuss the changes that occurred in the jar. How long did it take for the crystals to form? What shape are the crystals?

Workbook

Vocabulary Practice

Use vocabulary words in the crossword puzzle.

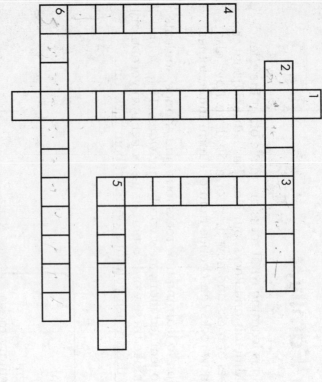

Across

2. material that settles at the bottom of lakes, rivers, and oceans
5. the way a mineral's surface reflects light
6. rocks that form when sediment cements together and hardens

Down

1. rocks that have changed as a result of heat and pressure
3. a natural crystal that makes up a rock
4. rocks that form from molten (melted) rock

© Pearson Education, Inc.

Know Your Rocks

Read each clue and circle the kind of rock it describes.

1. _____ is melted rock that is above ground.
   a. Lava
   b. Magma

2. _____ is melted rock that is below ground.
   a. Lava
   b. Magma

3. _____ rocks form from magma.
   a. Sedimentary
   b. Metamorphic
   c. Igneous

4. _____ rocks form from sediment that is pressed together.
   a. Sedimentary
   b. Metamorphic
   c. Igneous

Name _____

The Personal Vocabulary Journal shows vocabulary words you will see in this chapter. Fill in the second and third columns of the chart. After you finish reading the chapter, review your work to see how accurate your predictions were.

Personal Vocabulary Journal		
Vocabulary word	**How or where I have heard this word used before**	**What I think the word means**
deposition		
earthquake		
epicenter		
erosion		
fault		
landforms		
landslide		
volcano		
weathering		

Notes for Home: Your child learned the vocabulary terms for Chapter 9.
Home Activity: Choose a word from the list and have your child choose another word that is related to the first word and explain how the two words are related.

Name _____

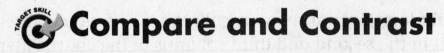
🎯 Compare and Contrast

Read the science article.

Gravity and Changing Landforms

We all know that gravity keeps us on Earth. But did you
know that gravity also plays a part in changing the
landforms on Earth? When a large amount of rock and
soil moves rapidly downhill, it is called a landslide. Heavy
rains or earthquakes loosen the material on a steep slope.
Gravity then pulls the loosened material downhill. When
a large amount of snow and ice moves rapidly down
a mountain, it is called an avalanche. Strong winds,
earthquakes, and explosions can trigger an avalanche.
Again, gravity is responsible for the snow and ice moving
quickly downhill. As you can imagine, both landslides
and avalanches can cause a great deal of damage.

Apply It!

Fill in the graphic organizer. List ways that a landslide and an avalanche are alike and different.

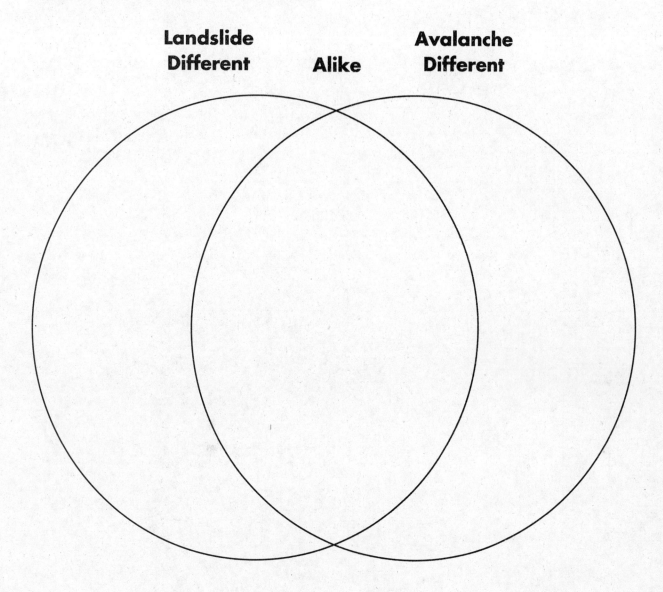

Landslide
Different

Alike

Avalanche
Different

Notes for Home: Your child learned how to compare and contrast two natural events.
Home Activity: Have your child choose two of his or her favorite activities and use a graphic organizer like the one above to compare and contrast them.

Notes

Name _____

Lesson 1: How does Earth's surface wear away?

Before You Read Lesson 1

Read each statement below. Place a check mark in the circle to indicate whether you agree or disagree with the statement.

	Agree	Disagree
1. Earth's crust covers about $\frac{2}{3}$ of its surface.	○	○
2. Some landforms form very quickly.	○	○
3. Melting ice is an example of weathering.	○	○
4. Chemical weathering changes the material that makes up a rock.	○	○

After You Read Lesson 1

Reread each statement above. If the lesson supports your choice, place a check mark in the *Correct* circle. Then explain how the text supports your choice. If the lesson does not support your choice, place a check mark in the *Incorrect* circle. Then explain why your choice is wrong.

	Correct	Incorrect
1. _____ _____	○	○
2. _____ _____	○	○
3. _____ _____	○	○
4. _____ _____	○	○

Notes for Home: Your child has completed a pre-/post-inventory of key concepts in the lesson.
Home Activity: Examine your backyard or another natural area and have your child point out examples of weathering.

Reviewing Terms: Sentence Completion

Complete each sentence with the correct word.

_____ 1. _____ are natural features on Earth's surface. (Oceans, Landforms)

_____ 2. The process that breaks down rocks in Earth's crust is called _____. (weathering, erosion)

Reviewing Concepts: Matching

Weathering is caused by many things. Match each factor with the type of weathering it causes. Write the letter on the line next to each description. You will use each answer more than once.

_____ 3. acids in rainwater

_____ 4. water freezing in cracks in rock

_____ 5. flowing water

_____ 6. temperature changes

_____ 7. chemicals from plants

_____ 8. ocean waves

a. physical weathering

b. chemical weathering

Writing

Use complete sentences to answer question 9. (2 points)

9. Write a description of one way that chemical weathering can change a rock.

_____

_____

_____

_____

_____

Lesson 2: How do weathered materials move?

Before You Read Lesson 2

Read each statement below. Place a check mark in the circle to indicate whether you agree or disagree with the statement.

		Agree	Disagree
1.	Erosion is a type of physical weathering.	○	○
2.	A delta is formed by deposition.	○	○
3.	Most glaciers move very quickly.	○	○
4.	Weathering can cause a landslide.	○	○

After You Read Lesson 2

Reread each statement above. If the lesson supports your choice, place a check mark in the *Correct* circle. Then explain how the text supports your choice. If the lesson does not support your choice, place a check mark in the *Incorrect* circle. Then explain why your choice is wrong.

		Correct	Incorrect
1.	_____	○	○
	_____		
2.	_____	○	○
	_____		
3.	_____	○	○
	_____		
4.	_____	○	○
	_____		

Notes for Home: Your child has completed a pre-/post-inventory of key concepts in the lesson.
Home Activity: Have your child explain to you what can be done to control erosion and explain why these actions are effective.

Reviewing Terms: Matching

Match each description with the correct word. Write the letter on the line next to each description.

_____ 1. the movement of weathered rock

_____ 2. the laying down of Earth materials

_____ 3. a rapid, downhill movement of rock and soil

a. erosion

b. landslide

c. deposition

Reviewing Concepts: Sentence Completion

Complete each sentence with the correct word.

_____ 4. A canyon is a landform caused by _____. (erosion, deposition)

_____ 5. Large ice sheets called _____ cause erosion as they move. (glaciers, landforms)

_____ 6. A _____ is formed by deposition. (delta, valley)

_____ 7. Gravity causes _____. (earthquakes, landslides)

_____ 8. Trees and plants can help reduce _____. (erosion, deposition)

Applying Strategies: Ordering Decimals

9. Deposition occurs when moving water slows down. Large particles are deposited before smaller particles. The diameters of five rocks are listed here: 2.3 cm, 1.8 cm, 1.2 cm, 1.9 cm, 2.1 cm
Write the diameters from the first to be deposited to the last to be deposited. (2 points)

Lesson 3: How can Earth's surface change rapidly?

Before You Read Lesson 3

Read each statement below. Place a check mark in the circle to indicate whether you agree or disagree with the statement.

		Agree	Disagree
1.	Plates moving along faults cause earthquakes.	○	○
2.	An extinct volcano is one that no longer exists.	○	○
3.	Some of Earth's landforms were created by earthquakes.	○	○
4.	Taller volcanoes produce more powerful eruptions.	○	○

After You Read Lesson 3

Reread each statement above. If the lesson supports your choice, place a check mark in the *Correct* circle. Then explain how the text supports your choice. If the lesson does not support your choice, place a check mark in the *Incorrect* circle. Then explain why your choice is wrong.

		Correct	Incorrect
1.	_____	○	○
	_____		
2.	_____	○	○
	_____		
3.	_____	○	○
	_____		
4.	_____	○	○
	_____		

Notes for Home: Your child has completed a pre-/post-inventory of key concepts in the lesson.
Home Activity: Have your child tell you how volcanoes and earthquakes are alike and how they are different.

Reviewing Terms: Matching

Match each description with the correct word. Write the letter on the line next to each description.

_____ 1. a cone-shaped landform that can erupt at times

_____ 2. a crack where Earth's crust can move

_____ 3. sudden movement that causes Earth's crust to shake

_____ 4. the point on Earth's surface directly above an earthquake's focus

a. fault

b. epicenter

c. volcano

d. earthquake

Reviewing Concepts: True or False

Write **T** (True) or **F** (False) on the line before each statement.

_____ 5. An active volcano is one that has not erupted in a long time.

_____ 6. Earth's crust is divided into plates.

_____ 7. The energy of earthquakes travels in waves.

_____ 8. Volcanic eruptions can affect Earth's climate.

Applying Strategies: Compare and Contrast

Use complete sentences to answer question 9. (2 points)

9. Describe one way that earthquakes and volcanoes are similar. Describe one difference between them.

_____

_____

_____

_____

_____

Name _____

Comparing Sizes of Earthquakes

The table lists the magnitudes of some earthquakes that
have recently occurred around the world.

Recent Earthquakes Worldwide			
Earthquake	Location	Date	Magnitude
A	Iran	Dec. 26, 2003	6.6
B	United States	Dec. 22, 2003	6.5
C	Japan	Sept. 25, 2003	8.3
D	Mexico	Jan. 22, 2003	7.6
E	India	Jan. 26, 2001	7.7
F	Turkey	Nov. 12, 1999	7.2

Use the table to answer the questions. Circle the letter of
the correct answer.

1. Where did the strongest earthquake listed occur?
    A. United States   C. Turkey
    B. Japan   D. India
2. Which shows the earthquakes listed in order from weakest to
    strongest?
    A. C, E, F, D, A, B   C. B, A, F, D, E, C
    B. A, B, D, E, F, C   D. B, A, D, E, C, F
3. Since 1900, the strongest earthquake ever had a magnitude of 9.5.
    What is the difference between this earthquake and earthquake C?
    A. 0.2   C. 2
    B. 1.2   D. 2.2
4. What is the range of the magnitudes listed?
    A. 3   C. 1.8
    B. 2.2   D. 1.2

Notes for Home: Your child learned how to compare and subtract decimal
numbers.
Home Activity: Write money amounts between $1 and $5 and have your child
compare and subtract the values.

Notes

Dear Family,

Your child is learning how Earth's surface is shaped and reshaped. In the science chapter Changes to Earth's Surface, our class has learned how rock on Earth's surface is broken apart, and why some landforms get bigger while others get smaller. Students have also learned what causes volcanoes and earthquakes.

In addition to learning about how Earth's surface changes, students have also learned many new vocabulary words. Help your child to make these words a part of his or her own vocabulary by using them when you talk together about changes to Earth's surface.

> landform
> weathering
> erosion
> deposition
> landslide
> volcano
> fault
> earthquake
> epicenter

The following pages include activities that you and your child can do together. By participating in your child's education, you will help to bring the learning home.

Family Science Activity
Making Volcanoes

This activity will help your child understand the forces that contribute to a volcanic eruption. The activity can get messy, so make sure you have plenty of space to work in and lots of paper towels to clean up with.

Materials:

- Plastic bottle
- Baking soda
- Dish detergent
- Vinegar
- Measuring cup
- Paper towels

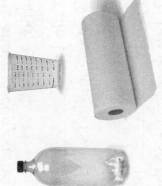

Steps

1. Discuss how volcanoes form and erupt. What comes out of a volcano? How does it come out?
2. Cover the bottom of the plastic bottle with baking soda. Then, add a small amount of dish detergent.
3. Fill the measuring cup with about 90 ml of vinegar.
4. Pour the vinegar into the bottle. The mixture will start to bubble.
5. Cover the top of the bottle with your hand. Shake the bottle a bit. You will feel pressure building. Wait 10–20 seconds.
6. Release your hand, stand back, and let the "lava" shoot out of the bottle. Use the paper towels to clean up the area.
7. Discuss how the pressure in the bottle is like the pressure in a magma chamber. By releasing your hand, you mimicked a crack in the Earth's crust. This is why "lava" shot out of the bottle.

Workbook

Vocabulary Practice

Find all of the vocabulary words from the chapter in the word search below.

Changes to Earth's Surface

```
G G N F G P I D N J T R Z O I
R N C L A N D F O R M S F M E
L X I L D K Z W I F K E O M P
J A A R W Q H O T P R N M N I
E O N C E O K Z I O U X L V C
T X D D C H G U S N F H U O E
V G Q G S R T I O T I Z V K N
N Z U A S L O A P J L C A N T
O X H R D N I J E R Q U I V E
O N A C L O V D D W Q N A S R
J J B U L I A S E H H F H F L
A N Y U F K G F T O N P T R G
E R X S U F N R N V C B P R H
N O C R X X A R H A W A O K K
S X P I Q E N V R U O N Q C H
```

Geology Guessing Game

Read the clues below. Each clue can be answered by only one of the vocabulary words. Write the answer on the line next to the clue.

1. I am a sudden movement that causes Earth's crust to shake. I can cause a lot of damage to a town or city.

   What am I? _____

2. I use water, ice, and wind to move weathered pieces of rock.

   What am I? _____

3. I am a break or crack in the rock where Earth's crust can move.

   What am I? _____

4. I am a rapid downhill movement of a large amount of rock and soil.

   What am I? _____

5. I use water, wind, ice, temperature, and chemicals to break rocks into smaller pieces.

   What am I? _____

ANSWERS: 1. earthquake; 2. erosion; 3. fault; 4. landslide; 5. weathering

Choose the correct vocabulary term to complete each sentence.

solar energy	humus	ore	fossil fuels
petroleum	conservation	recycling	

1. The energy that the Sun gives off is a renewable resource called

   _____.

2. _____ is finding uses for things instead of throwing them away.

3. Oil is the common name for _____.

4. _____ is a mineral-rich rock that is removed from Earth and used to make products.

5. The part of soil made up of decayed plant and animal matter is

   called _____.

6. _____ is the efficient use of resources.

7. _____ are made from the remains of organisms that lived long ago.

Notes for Home: Your child learned the vocabulary terms for Chapter 10.
Home Activity: Give your child clues to a vocabulary term and have him or her identify the term. For example, say, *"I can be doing this with paper, bottles, and cans."* (recycle) Provide clues for all terms.

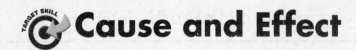

Cause and Effect

Read the paragraph below about how to reduce waste at school.

Reducing Waste

Recycling and composting can reduce waste. In 1999, these activities kept 64 million tons of waste from being burned in incinerators or buried in landfills. Here are three ways that you can reduce waste at school.

1   Carry your lunch in a reusable lunch bag or box. Put food in containers that you can wash. Because you are washing and reusing containers, you are creating less garbage.

2   Use refillable pens and pencils instead of disposable ones. Carry a well-constructed backpack that will last more than one year. By reusing items, you reduce waste.

3   Use less paper. Write on both sides of your notebook paper. Cut up paper written on one side and staple the blank sides together for scratch paper. Cutting back on your use of paper can result in producing far less trash.

Apply It!

Use the graphic organizer on page 93. Fill in the causes and effects from the article.

Effect	**Cause**
1. 64 million tons of material were not burned or buried as trash.	1. _____ _____ _____ _____
2. _____ _____ _____ _____	2. Use a lunchbox and reusable containers.
3. _____ _____ _____ _____	3. Carry a backpack that will last for more than one year.

Notes for Home: Your child learned how to identify the effects of reducing waste at school.
Home Activity: Brainstorm with your child a list of ways to reduce waste in your home.

Notes

Lesson 1: What are natural resources?

Before You Read Lesson 1

Read each statement below. Place a check mark in the circle to indicate whether you agree or disagree with the statement.

	Agree	Disagree
1. Petroleum is a renewable natural resource.	○	○
2. Erosion is a natural process so we do not need to worry about it.	○	○
3. Weathering helps to make soil a renewable resource.	○	○

After You Read Lesson 1

Reread each statement above. If the lesson supports your choice, place a check mark in the *Correct* circle. Then explain how the text supports your choice. If the lesson does not support your choice, place a check mark in the *Incorrect* circle. Then explain why your choice is wrong.

	Correct	Incorrect
1. _____	○	○
_____		
2. _____	○	○
_____		
3. _____	○	○
_____		

Notes for Home: Your child has completed a pre/post inventory of key concepts in the lesson.
Home Activity: Choose several items you use in your daily life and discuss with your child the resources used to produce and/or use the item.

Reviewing Terms: Sentence Completion

Complete the sentence with the correct word.

_____ 1. _____ energy is the energy given off by the Sun. (Nonrenewable, Solar)

_____ 2. The decomposing plant and animal remains in soil are called _____. (humus, minerals)

Reviewing Concepts: True or False

Write **T** (True) or **F** (False) on the line before each statement.

_____ 3. Natural resources can be living or nonliving.

_____ 4. Solar energy is a nonrenewable resource.

_____ 5. Soil is a renewable resource.

_____ 6. All soil is the same.

_____ 7. Clay soil is soil with large particles.

_____ 8. Plants grow well in soil that has lots of nutrients.

Applying Strategies: Cause and Effect

Use complete sentences to answer question 9. (2 points)

9. What is the effect of bacteria, fungi, worms, and insects making their home in the soil?

_____

_____

_____

Lesson 2: How are resources used for energy?

Before You Read Lesson 2

Read each statement below. Place a check mark in the circle to indicate whether you agree or disagree with the statement.

	Agree	Disagree
1. Wind is a renewable source of energy.	○	○
2. The energy in fossil fuels comes from the Sun.	○	○
3. It is easy to restore the trees in the forest.	○	○

After You Read Lesson 2

Reread each statement above. If the lesson supports your choice, place a check mark in the *Correct* circle. Then explain how the text supports your choice. If the lesson does not support your choice, place a check mark in the *Incorrect* circle. Then explain why your choice is wrong.

	Correct	Incorrect
1. _____	○	○
_____		
2. _____	○	○
_____		
3. _____	○	○
_____		

Notes for Home: Your child has completed a pre-/post-inventory of key concepts in the lesson.
Home Activity: Talk with your child about ways to conserve energy that comes from fossil fuels, such as walking to a nearby store instead of driving or by turning down the heat and wearing a sweater during the winter.

Reviewing Terms: Matching

Match each description with the correct word or phrase. Write the letter on the line next to each description.

_____ 1. a device that changes energy from the Sun into electrical energy

_____ 2. rock that is removed from Earth for the mineral resources it contains

_____ 3. fuel made from organisms that lived long ago

_____ 4. a fossil fuel that is also called oil

_____ 5. the practice of using only the resources you need

_____ 6. saving, collecting, or using material again

a. solar cell

b. fossil fuel

c. conservation

d. petroleum

e. recycling

f. ore

Reviewing Concepts: True or False

Write **T** (True) or **F** (False) on the line before each statement.

_____ 7. Flowing water can be used to generate electricity.

_____ 8. Mining fossil fuels has no effect on the environment.

Applying Strategies: Percentages

Rewrite the sentence below, but replace the boldface words with an equivalent percentage. (2 points)

9. More than **one half** of all aluminum cans sold are recycled.

_____

_____

Water Use in the United States

The circle graph below shows the estimated use of water
in the United States in 2000.

Estimated Use of Water in the United States in 2000

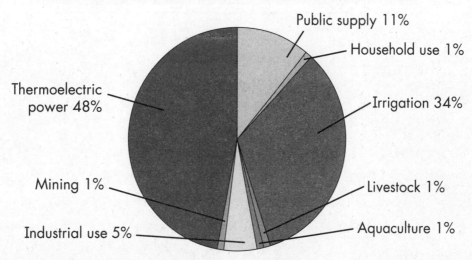

Public supply 11%

Household use 1%

Thermoelectric power 48%

Irrigation 34%

Mining 1%

Livestock 1%

Industrial use 5%

Aquaculture 1%

Use the graph above to answer the questions.

1. For what was most water used in the United States in 2000?
   A. mining
   B. irrigation
   C. household use
   D. thermoelectric power

2. About how much more of the total water used was used for
   irrigation than for household use?
   A. about 50% more
   B. about 10% more
   C. about 33% more
   D. about 1% more

3. Which two categories both used more water than public supply?
   A. irrigation and thermoelectric power
   B. industrial and irrigation
   C. domestic and mining
   D. mining and irrigation

4. About what percentage of water was used for thermoelectric power
   and irrigation combined?
   A. about 50 percent
   B. about 80 percent
   C. about 70 percent
   D. about 90 percent

Notes for Home: Your child learned how to interpret information in a circle
graph.
Home Activity: Identify the different ways that water is used in your household.
With your child, estimate the amounts used for each purpose and make a circle
graph to show how the family uses water.

Notes

Dear Family,

Your child is learning how living things can always have the natural resources they need. In the science chapter Using Natural Resources, our class has learned which energy sources are renewable and which are nonrenewable. The students have also learned how we can recycle materials and conserve energy.

In addition to learning what natural resources are, the students have also learned many new vocabulary words. Help your child to make these words a part of his or her own vocabulary by using them when you talk together about weather.

> solar energy
> humus
> solar cells
> ore
> fossil fuels
> petroleum
> conservation
> recycling

The following pages include activities that you and your child can do together. By participating in your child's education, you will help to bring the learning home.

© Pearson Education, Inc.

Family Science Activity
What Is Biodegradable?

Very often children are told about separating trash, recycling, and composting without knowing why these things are important. Putting food and plastic in a homemade compost bin helps to show why different materials have to be treated in different ways.

Materials

- milk carton
- dirt
- piece of plastic bag
- piece of lettuce
- water
- fork

Steps

1. Fill a milk carton halfway with dirt.
2. Put the lettuce and the plastic on top of the dirt.
3. Cover the lettuce and plastic with more dirt. Add 1 cup of water.
4. Place the milk carton in a safe place and wait several days.
5. Have your child predict if the trash will change or stay the same.
6. Use a fork to dig out the trash. Look at the lettuce and the plastic.
7. Discuss how the lettuce has changed but the plastic is the same.
8. Ask your child which item decomposes faster, food or plastic? Discuss composting, recycling, and how different types of garbage should be treated.

Workbook

Vocabulary Practice

Write the correct letter to match the vocabulary words with their meanings.

1. Solar energy _____

2. Humus _____

3. Ore _____

4. Fossil fuels _____

5. Conservation _____

6. Recycling _____

a. decaying plant and animal remains in soil

b. a mineral-rich rock deposit that can be removed from Earth

c. saving, collecting, or using materials again instead of turning them into waste

d. the energy given off by the Sun

e. energy sources including coal, natural gas, and oil that are made from the remains of living things that lived long ago

f. using only what you need as efficiently as possible

ANSWERS: 1. d; 2. a; 3. b; 4. e; 5. f; 6. c

Using Resources and Energy Sources

We use different kinds of resources to make products and to get energy. Renewable resources can be replaced. Nonrenewable resources cannot be replaced. Once you use them, they are gone. Write the name of each resource in the correct column below.

Renewable	Nonrenewable

1. Ore

2. Water

3. Soil

4. Petroleum

5. Wind

6. Fossil fuels

7. Sunlight

8. Natural gas

The Personal Vocabulary Journal below contains vocabulary words you will read in this chapter. For each word listed, record how or where you may have heard the word used before and then predict what you think the word means. After you read the chapter, review your work. Change any definitions, if necessary, and add any new information you learned.

Personal Vocabulary Journal			
Vocabulary word	How or where I have heard this word used before	What I think the word means	Changes or additional information
density			
mixture			
solution			
solute			
solvent			
solubility			
physical change			
chemical change			

Notes for Home: Your child learned the vocabulary terms for Chapter 11.
Home Activity: Have your child use the vocabulary words to explain the difference between a mixture and a solution.

Name _____

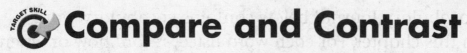

Use with Chapter 11.

Compare and Contrast

Students in a fourth grade science class conducted an experiment to observe what happens when water changes from a liquid to a gas. They wrote their observations in the lab report below. The report compares and contrasts liquid water and water vapor.

Lab Report

Procedure	Observations
We put some water in a dish and set it out in the Sun.	Water was liquid.
We left it in the Sun until all the water was gone.	There was a white substance left in the dish.

Interpret Results

Liquid water and water vapor are alike in some ways. Both are made of water molecules. When water gets warmed up, it evaporates into the air. It turns into a gas called water vapor, which becomes part of the air. You can't see water vapor in the air. Water vapor is less dense than liquid water, so it floats in the air. When water is a liquid, it expands to the size of its container. It does the same thing when it is a gas. Liquid water contains minerals, such as salt. However, the minerals do not evaporate. They are left behind when the water changes into a gas.

© Pearson Education, Inc.

Apply It!

Compare and contrast the liquid water and the water vapor in the activity. Complete the graphic organizer. Write at least two ways in which liquid water and water vapor are alike and at least two ways they are different.

Alike	Different

© Pearson Education, Inc.

Notes for Home: Your child learned how to compare and contrast substances.
Home Activity: Discuss with your child two of his or her favorite characters from a book or movie. Have your child use a chart to tell how the two characters are alike and different.

Notes

Lesson 1: What is matter?

Before You Read Lesson 1

Read each statement below. Place a check mark in the circle to indicate whether you agree or disagree with the statement.

	Agree	Disagree
1. All living and nonliving things are made of matter.	○	○
2. Water is the only substance that occurs naturally as a solid, a liquid, and a gas.	○	○
3. Any matter that takes the shape of its container is a liquid.	○	○
4. The particles in a solid are tightly packed together and do not move.	○	○

After You Read Lesson 1

Reread each statement above. If the lesson supports your choice, place a check mark in the *Correct* circle. Then explain how the text supports your choice. If the lesson does not support your choice, place a check mark in the *Incorrect* circle. Then explain why your choice is wrong.

	Correct	Incorrect
1. _____ _____	○	○
2. _____ _____	○	○
3. _____ _____	○	○
4. _____ _____	○	○

Notes for Home: Your child has completed a pre/post inventory of key concepts in the lesson.
Home Activity: Brainstorm with your child a list of substances and have your child identify each substance as a solid, a liquid, or a gas.

Reviewing Concepts: True or False

Write **T** (True) or **F** (False) on the line before each statement.

_____ 1. Liquids have a definite shape that does not change.

_____ 2. Solids have particles that can slide past one another.

_____ 3. Air is made up of gases.

_____ 4. Liquids take up a definite amount of space, but do not have a definite shape.

_____ 5. Gases have particles that move quickly and are far apart.

_____ 6. Liquids have closely-packed particles in fixed positions.

_____ 7. Ice is an example of a solid.

_____ 8. Liquids always fill their container.

Writing

Use complete sentences to answer question 9. (2 points)

9. Describe how you can use one of your senses to observe one property of matter.

_____

_____

_____

Name _____

Lesson 2: How is matter measured?

Before You Read Lesson 2

Read each statement below. Place a check mark in the circle to indicate whether you agree or disagree with the statement.

	Agree	Disagree
1. A person who weighs 100 pounds on Earth weighs 180 pounds on the Moon.	O	O
2. The volume of an object is the amount of space it takes up.	O	O
3. Density refers to how hard an object is.	O	O
4. Oil is more dense than water.	O	O

After You Read Lesson 2

Reread each statement above. If the lesson supports your choice, place a check mark in the *Correct* circle. Then explain how the text supports your choice. If the lesson does not support your choice, place a check mark in the *Incorrect* circle. Then explain why your choice is wrong.

	Correct	Incorrect
1. _____	O	O
_____		
2. _____	O	O
_____		
3. _____	O	O
_____		
4. _____	O	O
_____		

Notes for Home: Your child has completed a pre/post inventory of key concepts in the lesson.
Home Activity: Compare the densities of items in your home with the density of water by putting each item in water to see if it floats.

Name _____

Reviewing Terms: Sentence Completion

Complete the sentence with the correct word.

_____ 1. The amount of mass in a certain volume of matter is _____. (density, length)

Reviewing Concepts: Sentence Completion

Complete each sentence with the correct word or phrase.

_____ 2. A _____ is used to compare a mass that you know with one that you don't know. (pan balance, graduated cylinder)

_____ 3. The standard unit of mass in the metric system is the _____. (gram, liter)

_____ 4. Volume is the amount of _____ that matter takes up. (energy, space)

_____ 5. Cubic centimeters are units used to measure the _____ of solids. (length, volume)

_____ 6. An object's _____ determines whether it floats or sinks in water. (density, mass)

_____ 7. An ice cube is _____ dense that liquid water. (more, less)

_____ 8. If two solids have the same masses and different volumes, they have _____ densities. (different, equal)

Applying Strategies: Calculating

9. What is the volume of a cardboard box that is 12 cm long, 2 cm wide, and 3 cm high? Show your work. (2 points)

Lesson 3: How do substances mix?

Before You Read Lesson 3

Read each statement below. Place a check mark in the circle to indicate whether you agree or disagree with the statement.

	Agree	Disagree
1. In a mixture, all substances combine chemically with each other.	O	O
2. When you pour powdered lemonade mix into water, the water becomes a solvent.	O	O
3. If you pour sand into water, you make a solution.	O	O
4. You can dissolve more salt in warm water than you can in cold water.	O	O

After You Read Lesson 3

Reread each statement above. If the lesson supports your choice, place a check mark in the *Correct* circle. Then explain how the text supports your choice. If the lesson does not support your choice, place a check mark in the *Incorrect* circle. Then explain why your choice is wrong.

	Correct	Incorrect
1. _____	O	O
_____		
2. _____	O	O
_____		
3. _____	O	O
_____		
4. _____	O	O
_____		

Notes for Home: Your child has completed a pre/post inventory of key concepts in the lesson.
Home Activity: Have your child explain to you how a mixture and a solution are alike and how they are different.

Reviewing Terms: Matching

Match each description with the correct word. Write the letter on the line next to each description.

_____ 1. a combination of two or more substances

_____ 2. a mixture in which one substance dissolves in another

_____ 3. the substance that dissolves in a solution

_____ 4. the substance in a solution that dissolves another substance

_____ 5. a measure of the amount of a substance that will dissolve

a. mixture

b. solubility

c. solvent

d. solution

e. solute

Reviewing Concepts: True or False

Write **T** (True) or **F** (False) on the line before each statement.

_____ 6. The substances in a mixture are chemically combined.

_____ 7. The parts of a mixture can be separated.

_____ 8. A solute with small particles dissolves more quickly than one with large particles.

Applying Strategies: Compare and Contrast

Use complete sentences to answer question 9. (2 points)

9. What is one way that all mixtures are alike? What is one way that solutions are different from other mixtures?

_____

_____

_____

_____

_____

© Pearson Education, Inc.

Name _____

Lesson 4: How does matter change?

Before You Read Lesson 4

Read each statement below. Place a check mark in the circle to indicate whether you agree or disagree with the statement.

		Agree	Disagree
1.	When a solid melts, this is a phase change.	○	○
2.	Physical changes alter the matter's particles.	○	○
3.	A chemical change does not affect a substance's properties.	○	○
4.	The more energy a particle has, the faster the particles move.	○	○

After You Read Lesson 4

Reread each statement above. If the lesson supports your choice, place a check mark in the *Correct* circle. Then explain how the text supports your choice. If the lesson does not support your choice, place a check mark in the *Incorrect* circle. Then explain why your choice is wrong.

		Correct	Incorrect
1.	_____	○	○
	_____		
2.	_____	○	○
	_____		
3.	_____	○	○
	_____		
4.	_____	○	○
	_____		

Notes for Home: Your child has completed a pre/post inventory of key concepts in the lesson.
Home Activity: Discuss the preparation of different kinds of food and have your child identify the physical, chemical, and/or phase changes that take place.

Name _____

Reviewing Terms: Sentence Completion

Complete each sentence with the correct phrase.

_____ 1. A change in size, shape, or state of matter is a _____. (physical change, chemical change)

_____ 2. A change that produces a different kind of matter is a _____. (physical change, chemical change)

Reviewing Concepts: Matching

Match each description of a change in matter in the left column with the type of change in the right column. Write the letter on the line next to each description. You will use each answer more than once.

_____ 3. freezing

_____ 4. tarnishing

_____ 5. boiling

_____ 6. burning

_____ 7. dissolving

_____ 8. rusting

a. physical change

b. chemical change

Writing

Use a complete sentence to answer question 9. (2 points)

9. Write a sentence that describes the purpose of the Periodic Table.

_____

_____

_____

_____

© Pearson Education, Inc.

Name _____

Comparing Mass

The table below gives the masses of some common items. They have been rounded to the nearest tenth.

Object	Mass (in grams)
grape	1.2
dime	3.8
peanut	1.4
paper clip	1.0
pen cap	2.6

```
 1   1.2  1.4  1.6  1.8   2   2.2  2.4  2.6  2.8   3
 ├────┼────┼────┼────┼────┼────┼────┼────┼────┼────┤
 A    B    C                                  D
```

Use the graph to answer these questions.

1. Which point on the number line represents the mass of a grape?
   A. Point A   C. Point C
   B. Point B   D. Point D

2. Where on the number line would you plot the point for the mass of a dime?
   A. to the left of point A
   B. between point C and point D
   C. at point D
   D. to the right of point D

3. Which item weighs almost four times as much as a paper clip?
   A. grape   C. peanut
   B. dime   D. pen cap

4. If you arranged the items on the number line in order from least to greatest mass, what would be the correct order?
   A. peanut, grape, pen cap, paper clip, dime
   B. dime, pen cap, peanut, grape, paper clip
   C. paper clip, grape, peanut, pen cap, dime
   D. grape, peanut, paper clip, pen cap, dime

Notes for Home: Your child learned how to read and compare decimal numbers on a number line.
Home Activity: Help your child write several money amounts between one and two dollars. Then have your child arrange the amounts in order from least to greatest.

Notes

Dear Family,

Your child is learning how to identify and compare different states of matter. In the science chapter Properties of Matter, our class has learned the proper terms to describe states of matter. We have focused on how matter changes. Students have also learned how matter is measured and how matter can be combined physically and chemically.

In addition, students have also learned many new vocabulary words. Help your child to make these words a part of his or her own vocabulary by using them when you talk together about matter.

density
mixture
solution
solubility
solvent
solute
physical change
chemical change

The following pages include activities that you and your child can do together. By participating in your child's education, you will help to bring the learning home.

Family Science Activity
Exploring Density: Does It Float?

Materials:

- Glass of water
- Pencil
- Paper
- Household items, such as: a pen, a strip of paper, a rubber band, an eraser, an ice cube, a cork, a piece of fruit, some oil, some juice

Steps

1. Draw a chart with two columns. Label one column "Item" and the other column "Floats or Sinks?"

2. Ask your child to predict which items will float and which will sink in the glass of water.

3. One at a time, ask your child to drop each object in the water and observe if it floats or if it sinks. Help your child record these observations.

4. Discuss the results with your child. Which items floated? Which items sank? Why? Help your child compare these results to his or her predictions.

5. Encourage your child to find more items to drop into the water; add them to the chart.

Workbook

Vocabulary Practice

Circle the vocabulary words in the puzzle below.

chemical change	density	mixture	solubility
solute	solution	solvent	

```
Y  W  D  Q  O  E  F  L  B  D
W  T  J  V  T  C  A  E  A  E
L  E  I  U  Y  C  A  E  A  N
B  T  L  L  I  R  U  C  N  X
S  X  O  N  M  I  K  M  A  S
L  O  N  M  I  R  U  N  X  S
G  H  Z  H  V  B  M  B  O  I
S  O  T  D  J  L  Y  C  U  Y
C  G  T  V  B  U  C  H  Y  T
E  R  U  T  X  I  O  M  S  P
          T  I  O  N  P  O  B
                   M  S  P  S
```

Answers: chemical change, density, mixture, solubility, solute, solution, solvent

© Pearson Education, Inc.

Identifying States of Matter

What state is it in? For each item or substance, write if it is a solid, a liquid, or a gas.

ice _____

juice _____

smoke _____

paper _____

blood _____

air _____

eraser _____

water _____

car exhaust _____

steam _____

Fun Fact

Did you know that the element mercury is one of the only metals in the universe that can exist in liquid form at room temperature? Mercury freezes at −39°C and boils at 357°C. This is why mercury is used in many thermometers to measure temperature.

Answers: ice – solid, juice – liquid, smoke – gas, paper – solid, blood – liquid, air – gas, eraser – solid, water – liquid, car exhaust – gas, steam – gas

Workbook

Each of the vocabulary words for this chapter is shown below. For each sentence, unscramble the term in parentheses. Then use the word to complete the sentence.

thermal energy	conduction	conductor
insulator	convection current	radiation

1. _____ is energy due to moving particles that make up matter. (merhalt ryegen)

2. _____ is the transfer of heat energy by one thing touching another. (ocnutdonic)

3. A material that readily allows heat to move is a
_____. (rcootncdu)

4. A material that limits the amount of heat that passes through it is
called an _____. (ritonsaul)

5. A pattern of flowing heat energy is a _____.
(envoctcion trecrun)

6. Heat energy that travels through space from a light source, such as
the Sun, is called _____. (oidaranti)

Notes for Home: Your child learned the vocabulary terms for Chapter 12.
Home Activity: Help your child find examples of conductors, insulators, and radiation in your home.

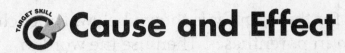

Cause and Effect

Visualize what you already know about how hot steam rises from a pan of boiling water. Read the conversation below.

Heating Air

Homeowner: I wish I understood how that radiator works.

Repair person: Well, it's based on some simple principles. The boiler in your basement heats water. As the water heats up, it turns to steam. This steam is pumped into pipes that run throughout your house. The pipes are connected to radiators in each room. The radiators are made of metal, such as cast iron, that allows the heat energy from the steam to pass through the walls of the radiator. Conduction, which is the transfer of heat energy by one thing touching another, warms the air in the room. The air is circulated around the room by convection currents.

Homeowner: What are convection currents?

Repair person: Convection currents form when air is heated and expands. Since it expands, it is less dense than the cooler air around it, so the cooler air sinks below the warmer air. As a result, the warm air is forced up, or rises. This pattern continues as long as there is cooler air above the radiator.

Apply It!

Use the graphic organizer below to identify an effect for each cause given.

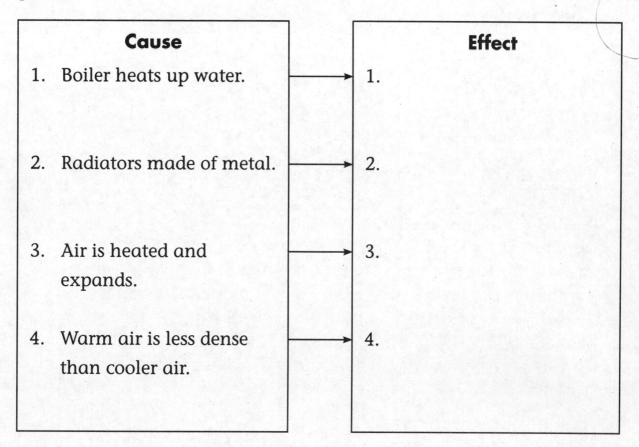

Cause	Effect
1. Boiler heats up water.	1.
2. Radiators made of metal.	2.
3. Air is heated and expands.	3.
4. Warm air is less dense than cooler air.	4.

Notes for Home: Your child learned how to identify cause-and-effect relationships.
Home Activity: Ask your child to use the illustrations in the chapter to explai
conduction, convection, and radiation to you.

Notes

Lesson 1: Why does matter have energy?

Before You Read Lesson 1

Read each statement below. Place a check mark in the circle to indicate whether you agree or disagree with the statement.

	Agree	Disagree
1. No energy is needed to change hot water to cool water.	○	○
2. Hot and cold water molecules move at the same speed.	○	○
3. A thermometer measures particle motion.	○	○
4. Heat is a measure of total energy.	○	○

After You Read Lesson 1

Reread each statement above. If the lesson supports your choice, place a check mark in the *Correct* circle. Then explain how the text supports your choice. If the lesson does not support your choice, place a check mark in the *Incorrect* circle. Then explain why your choice is wrong.

	Correct	Incorrect
1. _____ _____	○	○
2. _____ _____	○	○
3. _____ _____	○	○
4. _____ _____	○	○

 Notes for Home: Your child has completed a pre/post inventory of key concepts in the lesson.
Home Activity: With your child, use a thermometer to measure the temperature of an area near a sunny window, cold water from the tap, and warm tap water.

Reviewing Terms: Sentence Completion

Complete the sentence with the correct word or phrase.

_____ 1. Energy due to the moving particles that make up matter is _____. (thermogram, thermal energy)

Reviewing Concepts: True or False

Write **T** (True) or **F** (False) on the line before each statement.

_____ 2. Heat is the flow of thermal energy.

_____ 3. Temperature is the total energy in all of the particles in an object.

_____ 4. Temperature is measured using a thermometer.

_____ 5. Liquids expand when they are heated and contract when they are cooled.

_____ 6. The number of particles in an object affects its thermal energy but not its temperature.

_____ 7. A large pot of water and a small pot of water with the same temperature have the same thermal energy.

_____ 8. An object with a high temperature has particles that move quickly.

Applying Strategies: Comparing and Ordering Fractions and Decimals

9. Write the following temperatures in order, from least to greatest. (2 points)

$$25.6°C, \; 25\frac{1}{2}°C, \; 25.2°C, \; 25\frac{3}{4}°C$$

© Pearson Education, Inc.

Name _____

Lesson 2: How does heat move?

Before You Read Lesson 2

Read each statement below. Place a check mark in the circle to indicate whether you agree or disagree with the statement.

	Agree	Disagree
1. Heat moves through all matter at the same rate.	○	○
2. Warmer air sinks and cooler air rises.	○	○
3. There is heat energy in light.	○	○
4. Air is a fluid.	○	○

After You Read Lesson 2

Reread each statement above. If the lesson supports your choice, place a check mark in the *Correct* circle. Then explain how the text supports your choice. If the lesson does not support your choice, place a check mark in the *Incorrect* circle. Then explain why your choice is wrong.

	Correct	Incorrect
1. _____	○	○
_____		
2. _____	○	○
_____		
3. _____	○	○
_____		
4. _____	○	○
_____		

Notes for Home: Your child has completed a pre/post inventory of key concepts in the lesson.
Home Activity: Supervise your child as you test the insulating properties of utensils made of different materials in a pot of very hot water. Do not immerse the handles of the utensils.

Reviewing Terms: Matching

Match each description with the correct word or phrase. Write the letter on the line next to each description.

_____ 1. the transfer of heat energy by one thing touching another

_____ 2. a material that readily allows heat to move

_____ 3. a material that limits the amount of heat that passes through it

_____ 4. a pattern of flowing heat energy

_____ 5. energy that can travel through empty space or through matter

a. radiation

b. conduction

c. convection current

d. conductor

e. insulator

Reviewing Concepts: Sentence Completion

Complete each sentence with the correct word.

_____ 6. Wood and plastic are examples of _____. (conductors, insulators)

_____ 7. The air in a greenhouse is heated by_____. (conduction, radiation)

_____ 8. Thermal energy always moves from a warmer area to a _____ area. (cooler, hotter)

Applying Strategies: Cause and Effect

Use a complete sentence to answer question 9. (2 points)

9. What kind of heat transfer causes Earth's major wind patterns?

_____

_____

_____

Using Temperature Scales

The thermometer below uses the Celsius and Fahrenheit temperature scales. Use the thermometer to answer the questions.

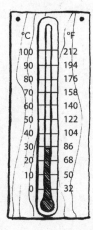

1. Water boils at 100°C. At what Fahrenheit temperature does water boil?

    _____

2. Water freezes at 32°F. At what Celsius temperature does water freeze?

    _____

3. The thermometer above is placed in a swimming pool. A swimmer reads the thermometer and states that the temperature is 28°. Is this 28°F or 28°C? How do you know?

    _____

    _____

4. An outdoor thermometer indicates it is 20° outside where people are ice-skating on a lake. Is this 20°F or 20°C? How do you know?

    _____

    _____

Notes for Home: Your child learned about Celsius and Fahrenheit temperature scales.
Home Activity: Find a thermometer with both scales on it and compare the Celsius and Fahrenheit measurements.

Notes

Dear Family,

In the science chapter Heat, our class learned the difference between heat and temperature. We also learned how heat is transferred through conduction, convection, and radiation. The students also learned about materials that are insulators and materials that are conductors.

In addition to learning about heat, the students also learned many new vocabulary words. Help your child to make these words a part of his or her own vocabulary by using them when you talk together about heat.

> thermal energy
> conduction
> conductor
> insulator
> convection current
> radiation

These following pages include activities that you and your child can do together. By participating in your child's education, you will help to bring the learning home.

Family Science Activity

Exploring Heat Transfer

Materials:

- two mugs
- water
- thermometer
- paper and pencil

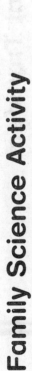

Steps

1. Help your child make a two-column chart. Label the first column "Boiling Water" and the second column "Ice Water."

2. Fill one mug with boiling water. Carefully place the thermometer in the water. Help your child to read the temperature on the thermometer and record the temperature on the chart.

3. Fill the other mug with ice water. Carefully place the cooled thermometer in the water. Help your child to read and record the temperature on the chart.

4. Approximately every 5 to 10 minutes, read and record the water temperatures until the two temperatures are the same.

5. Discuss with your child how thermal energy flows from something warm to something cool.

6. Together, identify what type of heat transfer occurred as the mugs of water changed temperature.

Workbook

Conductor or Insulator?

Look at the pictures of the materials.
Color the materials that are conductors.
Circle the materials that are insulators.

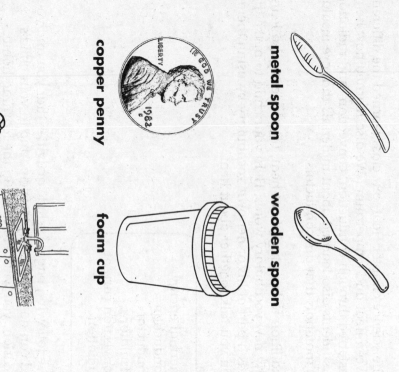

metal spoon

wooden spoon

copper penny

foam cup

iron bar

marble countertop

Heat Transfers

Read the clues on the cards for each type of heat transfer and then write in the type of heat on the line.

> This type of heat transfer occurs when one thing touches another. A pot on a stove is an example of this type of heat transfer.

> This type of heat transfer can travel through empty space or matter. The Sun transfers heat to Earth this way.

_____

_____

Fun Fact

The jet stream is a large convection current over North America. During the summer, the jet stream carries warm air from the southern United States all the way up into Canada. During the winter, the jet stream carries cold air from Canada all the way to Kentucky.

Answers: conduction; radiation

On the line, write the letter of the word or words that complete each sentence.

| static electricity | electric current | resistance | series circuit |
| parallel circuit | magnetism | magnetic field | electromagnet |

_____ 1. In a(n) _____, electrical current flows in one path only.
  A. parallel circuit   C. open circuit
  B. series circuit   D. closed circuit

_____ 2. In a(n) _____, electrical current has two or more paths to follow.
  A. parallel circuit   C. open circuit
  B. series circuit   D. closed circuit

_____ 3. _____ results when positive and negative charges no longer balance.
  A. An electric current   C. Static electricity
  B. A magnetic field   D. A negatively charged particle

_____ 4. A(n) _____ is an electric charge in motion.
  A. electric current   C. magnetic field
  B. electromagnet   D. closed circuit

_____ 5. _____ is the force that pushes or pulls magnetic materials near a magnet.
  A. Magnetic field   C. Resistance
  B. Electromagnetic   D. Magnetism

_____ 6. The invisible field around a magnet is the magnet's _____.
  A. resistance field   C. magnetic field
  B. electromagnet   D. electric current

_____ 7. A coil of wire wrapped around an iron core makes a(n) _____.
  A. electric current   C. magnetic field
  B. electromagnet   D. electric circuit

Notes for Home: Your child learned the vocabulary terms for Chapter 13.
Home Activity: Review the definitions of the vocabulary words with your child. Use the words in sentences that tell about ways your family uses electricity and magnetism.

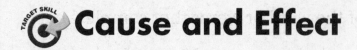
Cause and Effect

Heat From Lightning

What's much hotter than the surface of the Sun? The air around a lightning strike is. Lightning can really heat up a place. Here's what happens. The bottom of a storm cloud has negatively charged particles. These negatively charged particles move down toward the ground. They are attracted to positive charges there. As they move down, the positively charged particles rise to meet them. The movement of these particles produces an electric current, resulting in the flash of light that we call lightning. The lightning flash releases vast amounts of heat into the air. The air may become five times hotter than the surface of the Sun.

Apply It!

List causes and effects from the article in the graphic organizer on the next page.

Effect	Cause

$\longrightarrow$

Notes for Home: Your child learned how to identify cause-and-effect relationships.
Home Activity: With your child, list safety precautions to take during a thunderstorm. Post the list in your home.

Notes

Lesson 1: How does matter become charged?

Before You Read Lesson 1

Read each statement below. Place a check mark in the circle to indicate whether you agree or disagree with the statement.

		Agree	Disagree
1.	Everything in the universe is made of atoms.	○	○
2.	Electric energy can change into sound.	○	○
3.	Positively charged objects attract one another.	○	○
4.	A negative electric field attracts negative charges.	○	○

After You Read Lesson 1

Reread each statement above. If the lesson supports your choice, place a check mark in the *Correct* circle. Then explain how the text supports your choice. If the lesson does not support your choice, place a check mark in the *Incorrect* circle. Then explain why your choice is wrong.

		Correct	Incorrect
1.	_____	○	○
	_____		
2.	_____	○	○
	_____		
3.	_____	○	○
	_____		
4.	_____	○	○
	_____		

Notes for Home: Your child has completed a pre/post inventory of key concepts in the lesson.
Home Activity: Together with your child, experiment with static electricity by rubbing your feet quickly back and forth on a carpet and then touching something. Have your child explain static electricity after the experiment.

Reviewing Terms: Sentence Completion

Complete the sentence with the correct word or phrase.

_____ 1. _____ happens when positive and negative charges are not in balance. (Static electricity, Magnetism)

Reviewing Concepts: True or False

Write **T** (True) or **F** (False) on the line before each statement.

_____ 2. All atoms have a positive charge.

_____ 3. Moving charges generate electrical energy, which changes into sound, light, and heat energy.

_____ 4. Lightning happens because of the release of static electricity.

_____ 5. A charged object does not affect an object that has no charge.

_____ 6. The space around an electrically charged object is an electric field.

_____ 7. An electric field gets weaker the closer you get to the charged object.

_____ 8. A positive electric field repels a positively charged object.

Applying Strategies: Calculating

9. A bolt of lightning can get as hot as 50,000°F. Water boils at 212°F. How much greater is the temperature of lightning than boiling water? Show your work. (2 points)

© Pearson Education, Inc.

Name _____

Lesson 2: How do electric charges flow?

Before You Read Lesson 2

Read each statement below. Place a check mark in the circle to indicate whether you agree or disagree with the statement.

	Agree	Disagree
1. All electric charges are moving.	○	○
2. A parallel circuit has two or more paths for electric charge to follow.	○	○
3. Electric current flows the same in all materials.	○	○
4. Insulation prevents electric charges from leaving a wire.	○	○

After You Read Lesson 2

Reread each statement above. If the lesson supports your choice, place a check mark in the *Correct* circle. Then explain how the text supports your choice. If the lesson does not support your choice, place a check mark in the *Incorrect* circle. Then explain why your choice is wrong.

	Correct	Incorrect
1. _____	○	○
_____		
2. _____	○	○
_____		
3. _____	○	○
_____		
4. _____	○	○
_____		

Notes for Home: Your child has completed a pre/post inventory of key concepts in the lesson.
Home Activity: Show your child the circuit breakers or fuses used in your home. Discuss how they control the flow of electric current.

© Pearson Education, Inc.

Reviewing Terms: Matching

Match each description with the correct word or phrase. Write the letter on the line next to each description.

_____ 1. a moving electric charge

_____ 2. not allowing electric charge to flow easily

_____ 3. an electrical circuit with one path for electricity to follow

_____ 4. an electrical circuit with two or more paths for electricity to follow

a. series circuit

b. electric current

c. parallel circuit

d. resistance

Reviewing Concepts: Sentence Completion

Complete each sentence with the correct word.

_____ 5. Electric current travels _____. (slowly, quickly)

_____ 6. Electric current moves easily through _____ . (insulators, conductors)

_____ 7. In a circuit, electricity flows when the switch is _____. (open, closed)

_____ 8. The electric circuits in your school and home are _____ circuits. (series, parallel)

Applying Strategies: Compare and Contrast

Use complete sentences to answer question 9. (2 points)

9. Describe one similarity and one difference between series circuits and parallel circuits.

_____

_____

_____

_____

Name _____

Lesson 3: What are magnetic fields?

Before You Read Lesson 3

Read each statement below. Place a check mark in the circle to indicate whether you agree or disagree with the statement.

	Agree	Disagree
1. Magnetic minerals occur naturally.	○	○
2. Magnets have only north-seeking poles.	○	○
3. Earth's magnetic poles are located on its axis.	○	○
4. A compass always points to Earth's geographic North Pole.	○	○

After You Read Lesson 3

Reread each statement above. If the lesson supports your choice, place a check mark in the *Correct* circle. Then explain how the text supports your choice. If the lesson does not support your choice, place a check mark in the *Incorrect* circle. Then explain why your choice is wrong.

	Correct	Incorrect
1. _____	○	○
2. _____	○	○
3. _____	○	○
4. _____	○	○

Notes for Home: Your child has completed a pre/post inventory of key concepts in the lesson.
Home Activity: Using a compass, show your child how the instrument is used to determine direction.

Workbook

Think, Read, Learn **122**

Reviewing Terms: Matching

Match each description with the correct word or phrase. Write the letter on the line next to each description.

_____ 1. a force that pushes or pulls magnetic materials

_____ 2. the area around a magnet; strongest at the poles

a. magnetic field

b. magnetism

Reviewing Concepts: True or False

Write **T** (True) or **F** (False) on the line before each statement.

_____ 3. All magnetic fields have the same shape.

_____ 4. All magnets have two poles.

_____ 5. A magnet's poles all have the same charge.

_____ 6. Earth has a magnetic field.

_____ 7. Earth's magnetic poles and its geographic poles are in the same places.

_____ 8. Compasses work best when they are close to magnets.

Writing

Use complete sentences to answer question 9. (2 points)

9. Describe how a compass works.

_____

_____

_____

Lesson 4: How is electricity transformed to magnetism?

Before You Read Lesson 4

Read each statement below. Place a check mark in the circle to indicate whether you agree or disagree with the statement.

		Agree	**Disagree**
1.	An electromagnet uses a magnet to create electricity.	○	○
2.	Electric current creates a magnetic field.	○	○
3.	The strength of natural magnets can easily be increased.	○	○
4.	Electromagnets can be turned on and off.	○	○

After You Read Lesson 4

Reread each statement above. If the lesson supports your choice, place a check mark in the *Correct* circle. Then explain how the text supports your choice. If the lesson does not support your choice, place a check mark in the *Incorrect* circle. Then explain why your choice is wrong.

		Correct	**Incorrect**
1.	_____	○	○
	_____		
2.	_____	○	○
	_____		
3.	_____	○	○
	_____		
4.	_____	○	○
	_____		

Notes for Home: Your child has completed a pre/post inventory of key concepts in the lesson.
Home Activity: Have your child use the illustrations in the textbook to explain to you how an electromagnet works and how its strength can be increased.

Reviewing Terms: Sentence Completion

Complete the sentence with the correct word or phrase.

_____ 1. A coil wrapped around an iron core is an

_____. (electromagnet, electric compass)

Reviewing Concepts: True or False

Write **T** (True) or **F** (False) on the line before each statement.

_____ 2. Moving electric current causes a magnetic field.

_____ 3. An electromagnet has one pole.

_____ 4. There is more than one way to increase the strength of an electromagnet.

_____ 5. Making the core of an electromagnet larger makes the electromagnet weaker.

_____ 6. Electromagnets are used in doorbells.

_____ 7. Earphones change electric current to sound waves.

_____ 8. Electric motors change mechanical energy to magnetic energy.

Applying Strategies: Cause and Effect

Use a complete sentence to answer question 9. (2 points)

9. What is the effect of increasing the number of coils of wire wrapped around the core of an electromagnet?

_____

_____

_____

_____

Lesson 5: How is magnetism transformed to electricity?

Before You Read Lesson 5

Read each statement below. Place a check mark in the circle to indicate whether you agree or disagree with the statement.

	Agree	Disagree
1. All electric currents provide the same amount of energy.	○	○
2. Magnets can be used to produce electricity.	○	○
3. Electricity powers generators.	○	○
4. In a generator, mechanical energy spins wire around a magnet.	○	○

After You Read Lesson 5

Reread each statement above. If the lesson supports your choice, place a check mark in the *Correct* circle. Then explain how the text supports your choice. If the lesson does not support your choice, place a check mark in the *Incorrect* circle. Then explain why your choice is wrong.

	Correct	Incorrect
1. _____ _____	○	○
2. _____ _____	○	○
3. _____ _____	○	○
4. _____ _____	○	○

Notes for Home: Your child has completed a pre/post inventory of key concepts in the lesson.
Home Activity: Demonstrate how wind or falling water can make a pinwheel spin. Help your child relate the demonstration to the use of mechanical energy in a generator.

Reviewing Concepts: Sentence Completion

Complete each sentence with the correct word or phrase.

_____ 1. Changing a magnetic field generates _____.
(electricity, mechanical energy)

_____ 2. The slower the coils of an electromagnet
move, the _____ the current. (stronger,
weaker)

_____ 3. More coiled loops of wire around a magnet
make a _____ current. (weaker, stronger)

_____ 4. A generator uses wires and _____ to create
electricity. (batteries, magnets)

_____ 5. Michael Faraday and Joseph Henry
experimented with _____ (electricity,
chemistry)

_____ 6. A generator turns mechanical energy into
_____. (electrical energy, magnetic energy)

_____ 7. Electricity _____ dangerous. (is never,
can be)

_____ 8. Worn out or cracked electrical cords should
be _____. (relocated, replaced)

Writing

Use a complete sentence to answer question 9. (2 points)

9. Write a sentence that tells two different sources of energy that can
be converted to electricity by a generator.

_____

_____

_____

_____

Using Numbers to Represent Electrical Charges

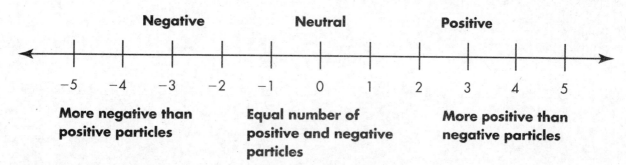

Negative   Neutral   Positive

−5 −4 −3 −2 −1 0 1 2 3 4 5

More negative than positive particles

Equal number of positive and negative particles

More positive than negative particles

Use the number line to answer these questions.

1. If some material has a charge of +6, what charge would make it neutral?
   A. +6   C. −6
   B. −3   D. −12

2. If a neutral piece of metal gains 5 negative charges and then loses 8 negative charges, what will its charge be?
   A. +3   C. +13
   B. −3   D. −13

3. If the air has a positive charge of 1 and your hair has a negative charge of 3, what will happen?
   A. Your hair will lay flat.
   B. Your hair will get curly.
   C. The air around your hair will become negatively charged.
   D. Your hair will stand straight up.

4. Balloon A has a negative charge of 3. Balloon B has a negative charge of 4. If both gain 2 positive charges, what will happen?
   A. Both will remain negatively charged.
   B. Both will become positively charged.
   C. Balloon A will become positively charged, but B will not.
   D. Balloon B will become positively charged, but A will not.

Notes for Home: Your child learned to use a number line.
Home Activity: Ask your child more questions about negative and positive charges. Have your child use the number line above to answer your questions.

Notes

Dear Family,

In the science chapter Electricity and Magnetism, our class has learned how objects become charged with electricity. We have also learned how electricity moves through circuits. The class studied how electricity and magnetism are related, and how magnetism can be transformed into electricity.

In addition to learning about electricity and magnetism, the students also learned many new vocabulary words. Help your child to make these words a part of his or her own vocabulary by using them when you talk together about electricity and magnetism.

> static electricity
> electric current
> resistance
> series circuit
> parallel circuit
> magnetism
> magnetic field
> electromagnet

The following pages include activities that you and your child can do together. By participating in your child's education, you will help to bring the learning home.

© Pearson Education, Inc.

Family Science Activity

Exploring Magnetic Force

Materials

- magnet
- paper clip

Steps

1. Have your child place the paper clip very close to the magnet. The paper clip will move toward the magnet.
2. Next, have your child place the paper clip far away from the magnet. This time, the paper clip will not move toward the magnet.
3. Have your child try several locations to see from how far away the paper clip will still be pulled toward the magnet.
4. Discuss with your child how this activity helps you to map the magnetic field of the magnet.

Workbook

Closed Circuits

Look at the diagram of the closed circuit.

Label each part of the circuit using words from the box.

Energy source	Means of energy transfer
Switch	Resistor

This does not allow electric current to flow easily through it. This resistance helps build up electric energy, which gives off heat and light.

The wires provide a path through which the charge flows.

When this is closed, the electric charge can flow.

This provides power for the circuit.

Magnetic Matching

Draw a line from the term in the left column to its definition in the right column.

magnetic field	when magnets push apart
magnetism	a coil of wire wrapped around an iron core
attract	the invisible area around a magnet
repel	when magnets pull together
electromagnet	the force that pushes or pulls magnetic materials near a magnet

Fun Fact

The first magnets used were actually stones. These stones were called lodestones and made of lead. Sailors often brought lodestones on ships to help magnetize compass needles to help stay on course.

Use the sentences to help you match each vocabulary word to its meaning. Write the letter of the definition on the line.

_____ 1. **wavelength:** The waves are close together, so their *wavelengths* are short.

_____ 2. **frequency:** *Frequency* refers to how often something happens in a certain amount of time.

_____ 3. **pitch:** Drums have a low *pitch*, and a whistle has a high *pitch*.

_____ 4. **reflection:** When you look in the mirror, you see your *reflection*.

_____ 5. **absorption:** The absorption of light energy makes a material warmer.

_____ 6. **transparent:** Glass is *transparent*.

_____ 7. **translucent:** A sheer curtain is *translucent*.

_____ 8. **opaque:** Wood is *opaque*.

_____ 9. **refraction:** *Refraction* made the pencil in the glass of water look broken.

_____ 10. **compression:** Compression is a pushing or squeezing together.

a. the bouncing back of a wave off an object or surface
b. materials that do not let any light pass through them
c. a measure of whether a sound seems high or low
d. the distance between a point on one wave and a similar point on the next wave
e. materials that let some light rays pass through but scatter some of the other rays
f. the taking in of light energy by an object
g. the part of the wave where the particles are closest together
h. the number of waves that pass a point in a certain amount of time.
i. the bending of light waves
j. materials that let nearly all the light rays that hit them pass through

Notes for Home: Your child learned the vocabulary terms for Chapter 14.
Home Activity: Look through your home for examples of as many of the vocabulary words as possible.

Draw Conclusions

Fireflies

On a summer's night, small, bright lights might be seen flashing through the air. Fireflies make these lights. Fireflies, or the common glowworm, are actually beetles. These beetles produce the lights through chemical reactions inside their bodies. They flash their lights in the darkness to attract mates. They also use their lights to warn enemies that they taste nasty and should be left alone! In some species only the male firefly has wings. The female cannot fly. However, males do not glow as brightly as females. At dusk, a female crawls up a grass stem or twig and waves her glowing tail at the sky.

Apply It!

Answer the questions on the next page by drawing conclusions from the article.

1. You see tiny lights flashing in the bushes on a warm summer's night. Draw a conclusion about what you see.

    _____

    _____

    _____

    _____

2. You see many brighter flashing lights in the grass. What can you conclude?

    _____

    _____

    _____

    _____

3. What might a predator do when they see the flashing lights of the common glowworm?

    _____

    _____

    _____

    _____

Notes for Home: Your child learned how to draw conclusions.
Home Activity: Read an article in a newspaper or magazine and help your child draw conclusions about the information.

Notes

Name _____

Lesson 1: What is sound energy?

Before You Read Lesson 1

Read each statement below. Place a check mark in the circle to indicate whether you agree or disagree with the statement.

		Agree	Disagree
1.	Sound is created when air vibrates.	○	○
2.	Sound waves carry sound energy.	○	○
3.	All sound waves carry the same amount of energy.	○	○
4.	All sound waves travel at the same speed.	○	○

After You Read Lesson 1

Reread each statement above. If the lesson supports your choice, place a check mark in the *Correct* circle. Then explain how the text supports your choice. If the lesson does not support your choice, place a check mark in the *Incorrect* circle. Then explain why your choice is wrong.

		Correct	Incorrect
1.	_____ _____	○	○
2.	_____ _____	○	○
3.	_____ _____	○	○
4.	_____ _____	○	○

Notes for Home: Your child has completed a pre/post inventory of key concepts in the lesson.
Home Activity: Speak into different materials, such as your hands, a piece of clothing, and a book. Have your child describe the difference in the sounds.

© Pearson Education, Inc.

Workbook

Reviewing Terms: Matching

Match each description with the correct word. Write the letter on the line next to each description.

_____ 1. the part of a sound wave where particles are bunched together

_____ 2. the number of waves that pass a point in a certain amount of time

_____ 3. the distance between the same point on one wave and a similar point on the next wave

a. wavelength
b. compression
c. frequency

Reviewing Concepts: Sentence Completion

Complete each sentence with the correct word.

_____ 4. Sound is a form of _____. (energy, matter)

_____ 5. Sound waves are _____ waves. (longitudinal, transverse)

_____ 6. The slower an object vibrates, the _____ the wavelength will be. (longer, shorter)

_____ 7. The type of matter that sound travels most quickly in is _____. (solid, liquid)

_____ 8. Echoes happen when sound waves hit an object and _____ back. (absorb, bounce)

Applying Strategies: Ordering Fractions

9. The wavelengths of several sound waves are listed below. Place the wavelengths in order from shortest to longest. (2 points)

$$3\frac{1}{2}\text{m}, 3\frac{2}{10}\text{m}, 3\frac{4}{5}\text{m}, 3\frac{2}{5}\text{m}$$

Name _____

Lesson 2: How is sound made?

Before You Read Lesson 2

Read each statement below. Place a check mark in the circle to indicate whether you agree or disagree with the statement.

	Agree	Disagree
1. Pitch is what makes a sound loud or soft.	○	○
2. Thicker guitar strings create a lower pitch.	○	○
3. You can change the pitch of a piano key by hitting it harder or softer.	○	○
4. Your inner ear is filled with liquid.	○	○

After You Read Lesson 2

Reread each statement above. If the lesson supports your choice, place a check mark in the *Correct* circle. Then explain how the text supports your choice. If the lesson does not support your choice, place a check mark in the *Incorrect* circle. Then explain why your choice is wrong.

	Correct	Incorrect
1. _____	○	○
_____		
2. _____	○	○
_____		
3. _____	○	○
_____		
4. _____	○	○
_____		

Notes for Home: Your child has completed a pre/post inventory of key concepts in the lesson.
Home Activity: Look through pictures of instruments. Discuss how a musician uses each instrument to make sound.

© Pearson Education, Inc.

Reviewing Terms: Sentence Completion

Complete the sentence with the correct word.

_____ 1. _____ is what makes a sound seem high or low. (Pitch, Loudness)

Reviewing Concepts: True or False

Write **T** (True) or **F** (False) on the line before each statement.

_____ 2. Loudness is related to the frequency of sound waves.

_____ 3. Your distance from a sound source affects how loud the sound seems.

_____ 4. Objects that vibrate quickly have a low frequency.

_____ 5. The thinnest strings on a violin play the highest notes.

_____ 6. Drums and maracas are percussion instruments.

_____ 7. The pitch of a wind instrument depends on the length of the column of air in the instrument.

_____ 8. Sound waves from the air travel on the auditory nerve to the brain.

Writing

Use a complete sentence to answer question 9. (2 points)

9. Write a sentence that describes the function of the outer ear.

_____

_____

_____

Lesson 3: What is light energy?

Before You Read Lesson 3

Read each statement below. Place a check mark in the circle to indicate whether you agree or disagree with the statement.

	Agree	Disagree
1. Unlike sound, light is a form of energy.	○	○
2. Light travels in straight lines.	○	○
3. We can see most of the universe's light energy.	○	○
4. The amount of moisture in the air affects the order of the colors in a rainbow.	○	○

After You Read Lesson 3

Reread each statement above. If the lesson supports your choice, place a check mark in the *Correct* circle. Then explain how the text supports your choice. If the lesson does not support your choice, place a check mark in the *Incorrect* circle. Then explain why your choice is wrong.

	Correct	Incorrect
1. _____ _____	○	○
2. _____ _____	○	○
3. _____ _____	○	○
4. _____	○	○

Notes for Home: Your child has completed a pre/post inventory of key concepts in the lesson.
Home Activity: Experiment with light with your child by changing the position and orientation of the light source as your child makes a shadow on the wall. Discuss your observations.

Name _____

Reviewing Concepts: True or False

Write **T** (True) or **F** (False) on the line before each statement.

_____ 1. Light and sound are both forms of energy.

_____ 2. Bioluminescence is Earth's most important source of light.

_____ 3. Light travels in straight lines.

_____ 4. Visible light is one form of electromagnetic radiation.

_____ 5. Microwaves are a form of visible light.

_____ 6. All electromagnetic waves can travel through empty space.

_____ 7. Radio waves are electromagnetic waves.

_____ 8. All electromagnetic waves have the same frequency.

Applying Strategies: Draw Conclusions

Use a complete sentence to answer question 9. (2 points)

9. If you are on the school playground and your shadow is very short, what can you conclude about the position of the Sun in the sky?

_____

_____

_____

Lesson 4: How do light and matter interact?

Before You Read Lesson 4

Read each statement below. Place a check mark in the circle to indicate whether you agree or disagree with the statement.

	Agree	Disagree
1. All objects reflect light waves.	O	O
2. Absorption changes light energy into heat energy.	O	O
3. Red glass only reflects and transmits red light waves.	O	O
4. The pupil of your eye is a muscle.	O	O

After You Read Lesson 4

Reread each statement above. If the lesson supports your choice, place a check mark in the *Correct* circle. Then explain how the text supports your choice. If the lesson does not support your choice, place a check mark in the *Incorrect* circle. Then explain why your choice is wrong.

	Correct	Incorrect
1. _____	O	O
_____		
2. _____	O	O
_____		
3. _____	O	O
_____		
4. _____	O	O
_____		

Notes for Home: Your child has completed a pre/post inventory of key concepts in the lesson.
Home Activity: Shine light from a flashlight through different materials. Have your child tell whether the material is transparent, translucent, or opaque.

Reviewing Terms: Sentence Completion

Complete each sentence with the correct word.

_____ 1. _____ occurs when light rays bounce off a surface and back to your eyes. (Absorption, Reflection)

_____ 2. _____ is when light rays are taken in by an object. (Absorption, Reflection)

_____ 3. A material that transmits almost all light is called _____. (translucent, transparent)

_____ 4. A material that lets some, but not all, light pass is called _____. (opaque, translucent)

_____ 5. _____ material does not let any light pass through. (Transparent, Opaque)

_____ 6. During _____, light rays are bent. (reflection, refraction)

Reviewing Concepts: True or False

Write **T** (True) or **F** (False) on the line before each statement.

_____ 7. A green apple appears green because it reflects light waves of the green frequency.

_____ 8. A convex lens is thicker at the edges than in the middle.

Writing

Use a complete sentence to answer question 9. (2 points)

9. Write a sentence that describes one way that people use lasers.

_____

_____

_____

© Pearson Education, Inc.

Comparing the Speed of Light

The speed of light in a vacuum is 299,792,458 meters per second. When you hear people talk about the speed of light, they are usually referring to this measurement—that is, the speed of light in a vacuum. The actual speed of light, however, depends on the material that the light moves through. For example, light moves slower in water, in glass, and through the atmosphere than it does through a vacuum. The bar graph below shows the speed of light in a vacuum and other mediums.

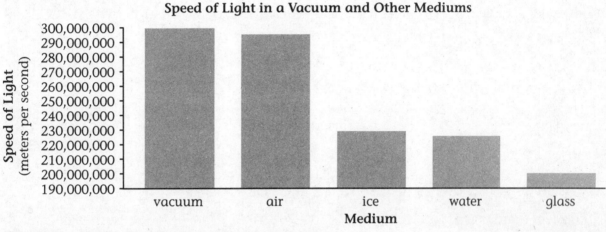

Use the graph to answer these questions.

1. Through which on the mediums does light travel the slowest? How do you know?

   _____

   _____

2. Does light travel faster through ice or water? How do you know?

   _____

   _____

3. Light travels fastest through a vacuum. Through which medium does it travel at the next fastest speed. How do you know?

   _____

   _____

   _____

Notes for Home: Your child learned how to read a bar graph.
Home Activity: Look for bar graphs in a newspaper or magazine. Have your child explain the data displayed in the graphs.

Notes

Dear Family,

In the science chapter Sound and Light, our class learned how sound energy travels in waves at different speeds through different mediums. We have also learned how sound is made by studying how musical instruments make sound. The students also explored sources of light energy and the electromagnetic spectrum. Further, students studied how light behaves when it strikes matter.

In addition to learning about sound and light, the students also learned many new vocabulary words. Help your child to make these words a part of his or her own vocabulary by using them when you talk together about sound and light.

compression
frequency
wavelength
pitch
reflection
absorption
transparent
translucent
opaque
refraction

The following pages include activities that you and your child can do together. By participating in your child's education, you will help to bring the learning home.

Family Science Activity

Exploring Pitch

Materials:

- 2 large rubber bands
- 2 plastic containers, 1 large, 1 small

Steps

1. Wrap a rubber band around each container.
2. Have your child pluck each rubber band and note the vibration of the rubber band and the pitch of the sound created.
3. Discuss with your child how the rubber band on the larger container had a faster vibration and higher pitch than the rubber band on the smaller container.
4. You may discuss musical instruments such as the guitar, piano, violin, and harp. Ask your child how these instruments make sounds. How do they make higher and lower pitched sounds? (with strings that are stretched tightly or loosely)

Workbook

How Will Light Behave?

Look at the pictures of the materials.
Draw a line from the material to the description of how light will behave when it strikes the material.

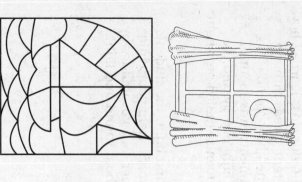

No light will pass through this material.

Almost all light will pass through this material.

Some light will pass through this material.

How Sound Travels

A scientist created a sound that traveled through three different mediums.

Write 1, 2, and 3 on the lines.

1 is for the medium the sound travels fastest through.

2 is for the medium the sound travels a little slower through.

3 is for the medium the sound travels slowest through.

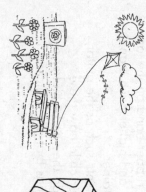

Air

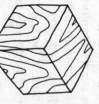

Wood Block

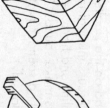

Swimming Pool

Fun Fact

Special machines on spacecraft, like *Cassini-Huygens*, can actually "see" wavelengths in the electromagnetic spectrum. These machines help spacecraft study other objects in space.

Answers: 3, 1, 2

Read each vocabulary word and its definition. Then use what you learned to complete each sentence with the correct vocabulary word.

relative motion: the change in one object's position compared to another object's fixed position
frame of reference: the objects you use to detect motion
speed: the rate at which an object changes position
velocity: both the speed and direction of a moving object
force: any push or pull
friction: a force that acts when two surfaces rub together
gravity: a force with makes objects pull toward each other
work: the ability to move something
kinetic energy: the energy of motion
potential energy: stored energy

1. The _____ of a plane is different when it takes off than when it lands.

2. How an object seems to move depends on your _____ _____.

3. _____ is the energy used to pick up a package.

4. You create _____ when you rub your hands together to keep them warm.

5. A swing going back and forth has _____.

6. Whether an object is moving or not depends on its _____ _____.

7. A stretched rubber band has _____.

8. The _____ of sound is 1,190 kilometers per hour.

9. _____ keeps us from floating away into space.

10. It takes a lot of _____ to stop an airplane.

Notes for Home: Your child learned the vocabulary terms for Chapter 15.
Home Activity: Discuss how the terms above relate to various activities such as riding a bike, pushing a piece of furniture, squeezing juice from fruit, and flying a kite.

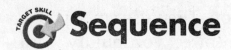
Sequence

Read the investigation about gravity below.

Procedure

The purpose of the following investigation is to demonstrate that gravity pulls all things down at the same speed. Begin by holding a piece of paper in one hand and a book in the other. Then, drop the book and the paper at the same time. Observe the paper and book as they fall and strike the floor. Next, place the paper on top of the book. Do not have any of the paper hanging over the edges of the book. Finally, hold the book waist high and drop it. Observe the paper and book as they fall and strike the floor.

Apply It!

Ask questions to help you remember the order in which the steps of the investigation take place. Write your questions on page 141.

© Pearson Education, Inc.

Write three questions that you might ask your classmates about the sequence of events.

1. _____
   _____
   _____
   _____

2. _____
   _____
   _____
   _____

3. _____
   _____
   _____
   _____

© Pearson Education, Inc.

Notes for Home: Your child learned how to sequence the events of an investigation.
Home Activity: Make a sandwich with your child. Ask your child to use the terms *first, next, then,* and *last* to describe the steps used to make the sandwich.

Notes

Lesson 1: What is motion?

Before You Read Lesson 1

Read each statement below. Place a check mark in the circle to indicate whether you agree or disagree with the statement.

	Agree	Disagree
1. Vibration is a circular motion.	○	○
2. Movement is determined by your frame of reference.	○	○
3. You always accelerate when you turn the corner on your bike.	○	○
4. Velocity is a measure of change in direction.	○	○

After You Read Lesson 1

Reread each statement above. If the lesson supports your choice, place a check mark in the *Correct* circle. Then explain how the text supports your choice. If the lesson does not support your choice, place a check mark in the *Incorrect* circle. Then explain why your choice is wrong.

	Correct	Incorrect
1. _____	○	○
_____		
2. _____	○	○
_____		
3. _____	○	○
_____		
4. _____	○	○
_____		

Notes for Home: Your child has completed a pre/post inventory of key concepts in the lesson.
Home Activity: Discuss situations, such as riding in a car versus watching it go by, in which your frame of reference affects how you perceive if an object is moving.

Reviewing Terms: Matching

Match each description with the correct word or phrase. Write the letter on the line next to each description.

_____ 1. one object's motion as compared to an object in a fixed position

_____ 2. the objects used to detect motion

_____ 3. the rate at which an object changes position

_____ 4. the speed and direction in which an object is moving

a. relative motion

b. velocity

c. frame of reference

d. speed

Reviewing Concepts: Sentence Completion

Complete each sentence with the correct word or phrase.

_____ 5. Objects can move in _____. (one way, several ways)

_____ 6. To find an object's average speed, you need to know the distance traveled and the _____. (time, direction)

_____ 7. *North, south, east,* and *west* are words used to describe an object's _____. (speed, velocity)

_____ 8. Any change in speed or direction of motion is _____. (acceleration, velocity)

Applying Strategies: Calculating

9. What is the average speed in kilometers per hour of a car that travels 240 kilometers in 4 hours? Show your work. (2 points)

Name _____

Lesson 2: How does force affect moving objects?

Before You Read Lesson 2

Read each statement below. Place a check mark in the circle to indicate whether you agree or disagree with the statement.

	Agree	Disagree
1. A force must touch an object to move it.	◯	◯
2. Balanced forces cancel each other.	◯	◯
3. Less force is needed to change the motion of an object with greater mass.	◯	◯
4. Friction can change the speed of moving objects.	◯	◯

After You Read Lesson 2

Reread each statement above. If the lesson supports your choice, place a check mark in the *Correct* circle. Then explain how the text supports your choice. If the lesson does not support your choice, place a check mark in the *Incorrect* circle. Then explain why your choice is wrong.

	Correct	Incorrect
1. _____	◯	◯
_____		
2. _____	◯	◯
_____		
3. _____	◯	◯
_____		
4. _____	◯	◯
_____		

Notes for Home: Your child has completed a pre/post inventory of key concepts in the lesson.
Home Activity: Discuss with your child how the brakes on a bicycle use friction to slow the bicycle down.

Reviewing Terms: Sentence Completion

Complete each sentence with the correct word.

_____ 1. _____ is any push or pull. (Force, Motion)

_____ 2. _____ is a force that acts when two surfaces rub together. (Friction, Magnetism)

Reviewing Concepts: True or False

Write **T** (True) or **F** (False) on the line before each statement.

_____ 3. Magnetism is a force that acts only on contact.

_____ 4. A strong magnet will cause a larger change in motion than a weak magnet.

_____ 5. Balanced forces change an object's motion.

_____ 6. Forces can be combined.

_____ 7. Rough surfaces exert more friction than smooth surfaces.

_____ 8. An object's weight affects the amount of friction between the object and a surface.

Writing

Use a complete sentence to answer question 9. (2 points)

9. Write a sentence that defines the term *inertia*.

_____

_____

_____

Name _____

Think, Read, Learn

Use with pages 446–449.

Lesson 3: How are force, mass, and energy related?

Before You Read Lesson 3

Read each statement below. Place a check mark in the circle to indicate whether you agree or disagree with the statement.

	Agree	Disagree
1. Gravity is the force that makes two objects pull toward each other.	O	O
2. Kilometers are the units of force scientists use.	O	O
3. Potential energy is the energy of motion.	O	O
4. Energy cannot be destroyed or made.	O	O

After You Read Lesson 3

Reread each statement above. If the lesson supports your choice, place a check mark in the *Correct* circle. Then explain how the text supports your choice. If the lesson does not support your choice, place a check mark in the *Incorrect* circle. Then explain why your choice is wrong.

	Correct	Incorrect
1. _____	O	O
_____		
2. _____	O	O
_____		
3. _____	O	O
_____		
4. _____	O	O
_____		

Notes for Home: Your child has completed a pre/post inventory of key concepts in the lesson.
Home Activity: With your child, use a pendulum clock or outdoor swing to demonstrate and discuss kinetic and potential energy.

© Pearson Education, Inc.

Workbook

Think, Read, Learn **144**

Reviewing Terms: Matching

Match each description with the correct word or phrase. Write the letter on the line next to each description.

_____ 1. a force that makes objects pull toward each other

_____ 2. the ability to move something

_____ 3. the energy of motion

_____ 4. stored energy

a. work

b. kinetic energy

c. potential energy

d. gravity

Reviewing Concepts: Sentence Completion

Complete each sentence with the correct word.

_____ 5. The gravity between two objects depends on mass and _____. (volume, distance)

_____ 6. _____ is the measure of the force of gravity acting on an object. (Mass, Weight)

_____ 7. The unit of force is the _____. (gram, newton)

_____ 8. _____ is the ability to do work. (Energy, Matter)

Applying Strategies: Sequence

9. The steps of an energy change are listed below, but they are out of order. Use the clue words to write the sentences in the correct order. (2 points)

Then energy is changed to kinetic energy as the animal moves.
First, plants store the Sun's energy as potential energy.
Next, animals eat the plants.

_____

_____

_____

_____

Name _____

Math in Science

Use with Chapter 15.

Relating Weights on Earth and on the Moon

Because the Moon has less mass than Earth, it has a smaller gravitational effect. On the surface of the Moon, the level of gravity is only about one-sixth of that on Earth. You can use the formula below to find the approximate weight of an object on the Moon.

$$\text{weight on Earth} \times \frac{1}{6} = \text{weight on the Moon}$$

If you weigh 66 pounds on Earth, you can use the formula to find your weight on the Moon.

$$66 \times \frac{1}{6} = 11$$

So, you would weigh about 11 pounds on the Moon.

Use the formula to complete the chart.

Item	Approximate Weight on Earth	Approximate weight on the Moon
a sack of apples	6 pounds	
small dog	18 pounds	
a small child	36 pounds	
an adult human	210 pounds	
a large refrigerator	600 pounds	
a car	2,400 pounds	
a whale	42,000 pounds	

Notes for Home: Your child learned how to use a formula to find the approximate weight of objects on the Moon.
Home Activity: Help your child use the formula to find the Moon weight of family members.

© Pearson Education, Inc.

Workbook

Math in Science **145**

Notes

Dear Family,

Your child is learning how things around them move in different ways. In the science chapter Objects in Motion, our class learned how to describe and measure motion. We focused on how forces affect the motion of objects. Students also learned how force, motion, and energy are related.

In addition, students also learned many new vocabulary words. Help your child to make these words a part of his or her own vocabulary by using them when you talk together about motion.

relative motion
frame of reference
speed
velocity
force
friction
gravity
work
kinetic energy
potential energy

The following pages include activities that you and your child can do together. By participating in your child's education, you will help to bring the learning home.

Family Science Activity

Exploring Potential Energy

Materials:

- four books
- cardboard
- paper cup
- a marble (or similar sized ball)
- ruler
- paper and pencil

Steps

1. Make a ramp using one book and the piece of cardboard. Place a paper cup on its side at the bottom of the ramp.

2. Have your child place the marble at the top of the ramp and release it. The marble should roll into the paper cup.

3. Using a ruler, measure the distance the cup moved. Write this measurement on a piece of paper.

4. Add another book to the ramp to make it steeper. Repeat the activity. Continue adding books to the ramp until all four books have been used.

5. Compare the distances. Discuss how the marble that rolled down the highest ramp had the greatest amount of potential energy.

Workbook

Vocabulary

Unscramble the words. Then match them to their definitions.

oferc _____   a combination of both the speed and the direction an object is moving

krow _____   the rate at which an object changes position

yleovtci _____   the ability to move something

niietck gyneer _____ any push or pull

tiifonrc _____   a force that acts when two surfaces rub together

dsepe _____   energy of motion

teevrlai omtnoi _____ a force that makes objects pull toward each other

atryivg _____   the change in one object's position compared to another object's fixed position

Force and Mass

Look at the pictures. Circle the picture that would take the most force to move. Use the word *mass* to explain why you circled that picture.

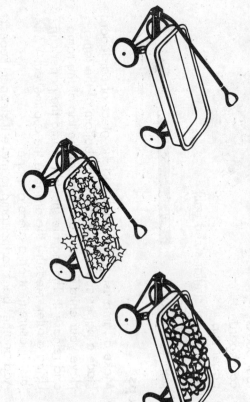

Fun Fact

Did you know that Earth's gravity keeps the Moon in orbit around Earth? However, the Moon's gravity also pulls on Earth. We can see proof of this during high and low tides. The Moon's gravity is strong enough to move Earth's water.

Use the vocabulary words in the box to complete the paragraphs.

effort	fulcrum	inclined plane	lever	load
pulley	screw	wedge	wheel and axle	

A _____ is a long bar with a support. The support is called the _____. The lever is used to lift or move a _____. When using a lever, you put in _____ to make the load move. A _____ is a two-part simple tool used to turn objects. A _____ is a wheel with a rope, wire, or chain around it that can change the direction of force. Two pulleys used together can also cut down on the amount of force needed to lift a load.

In science, a ramp is called an _____. The slope of the ramp changes the amount of force needed to move an object. A _____ is actually a special kind of inclined plane. Applied force can drive the thin edge of the wedge deep into an object. Another type of inclined plane is a _____, which is used to hold things together, such as wood.

Notes for Home: Your child learned the vocabulary terms for Chapter 16.
Home Activity: Look around your home for examples of simple machines described above, such as a nutcracker, can opener, hammer, and window shade.

TARGET SKILL ⊙ Summarize

Read the paragraph describing screws below.

Screws

The screw is a simple machine that is a winding *inclined plane*.
If you hold a screw in two fingers and turn it, you can feel the
ridges spiral. The closer together the ridges, or threads, of a screw
are, the easier the screw turns. People use screws to connect
things, such as two pieces of wood. Screws can also be used with
other simple machines. A jackscrew combines a screw with a
lever. The jackscrew can easily lift a car. Screws and other simple
machines can make jobs easier to do.

Apply It!

Use the graphic organizer on the next page to choose ideas for a
summary of the paragraph about screws. Then write one or two
sentences to summarize the paragraph.

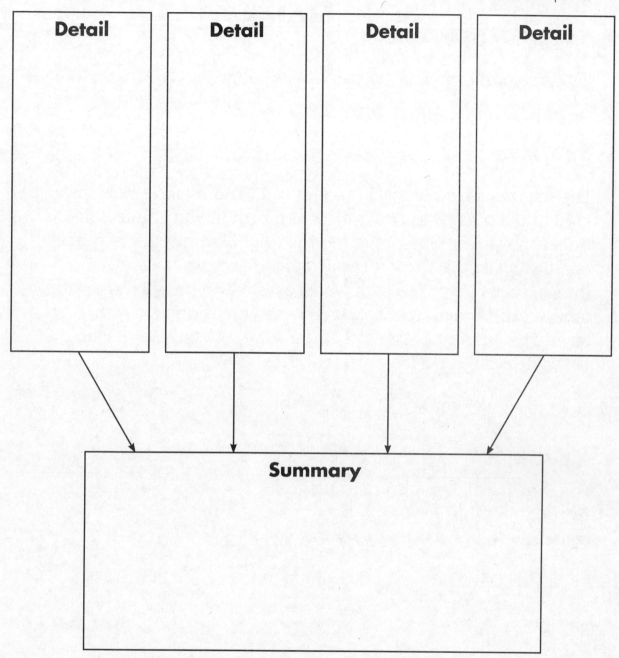

Detail

Detail

Detail

Detail

Summary

🎒 **Notes for Home:** Your child learned how to summarize information.
Home Activity: Explain to your child how to do a simple activity, such as make a bed. Then have your child summarize the process for you.

Notes

Lesson 1: What is a machine?

Before You Read Lesson 1

Read each statement below. Place a check mark in the circle to indicate whether you agree or disagree with the statement.

		Agree	Disagree
1.	In science, *work* means to push or pull to change the motion of something.	○	○
2.	Levers are used to apply force.	○	○
3.	The fulcrum is a point halfway between the effort and the load.	○	○
4.	A pulley changes the direction of the force.	○	○

After You Read Lesson 1

Reread each statement above. If the lesson supports your choice, place a check mark in the *Correct* circle. Then explain how the text supports your choice. If the lesson does not support your choice, place a check mark in the *Incorrect* circle. Then explain why your choice is wrong.

		Correct	Incorrect
1.	_____	○	○
	_____		
2.	_____	○	○
	_____		
3.	_____	○	○
	_____		
4.	_____	○	○
	_____		

Notes for Home: Your child has completed a pre/post inventory of key concepts in the lesson.
Home Activity: Look for examples of items in your home that make use of simple machines such as levers, fulcrums, wheel and axles, and pulleys.

© Pearson Education, Inc.

Reviewing Terms: Matching

Match each description with the correct word or phrase. Write the letter on the line next to each description.

_____ 1. a long bar with a support

_____ 2. the support in a lever

_____ 3. an object that is moved or lifted by a lever

_____ 4. a push or a pull on a lever that moves the load

_____ 5. a special kind of lever that turns objects

_____ 6. a wheel with a rope, wire, or chain around it

a. effort

b. lever

c. pulley

d. load

e. wheel and axle

f. fulcrum

Reviewing Concepts: Sentence Completion

Complete each sentence with the correct word.

_____ 7. One example of a lever is a _____. (wedge, wheelbarrow)

_____ 8. A _____ is an example of a wheel and axle. (screwdriver, nutcracker)

Writing

Use a complete sentence to answer question 9. (2 points)

9. Write a sentence that describes the way levers are classified.

_____

_____

_____

_____

© Pearson Education, Inc.

Lesson 2: How can machines work together?

Before You Read Lesson 2

Read each statement below. Place a check mark in the circle to indicate whether you agree or disagree with the statement.

	Agree	Disagree
1. It takes less force to push an object up a hill than to lift it straight up.	O	O
2. Rubbing your hands together produces friction.	O	O
3. A thumbtack is not an inclined plane.	O	O
4. A complex machine is made of simple machines.	O	O

After You Read Lesson 2

Reread each statement above. If the lesson supports your choice, place a check mark in the *Correct* circle. Then explain how the text supports your choice. If the lesson does not support your choice, place a check mark in the *Incorrect* circle. Then explain why your choice is wrong.

	Correct	Incorrect
1. _____	O	O
_____		
2. _____	O	O
_____		
3. _____	O	O
_____		
4. _____	O	O
_____		

Notes for Home: Your child has completed a pre/post inventory of key concepts in the lesson.
Home Activity: Look at pictures of complex machines and have your child identify the simple machines that are used in it.

Reviewing Terms: Sentence Completion

Complete each sentence with the correct word or phrase.

_____ 1. A ramp is a simple machine called a(n)
_____. (screw, inclined plane)

_____ 2. Two inclined planes put together form a(n)
_____. (auger, wedge)

_____ 3. An inclined plane wrapped in a circle is a
_____. (screw, wedge)

Reviewing Concepts: True or False

Write **T** (True) or **F** (False) on the line before each statement.

_____ 4. An inclined plane increases the distance over which a force is applied.

_____ 5. Friction makes objects move faster over an inclined plane.

_____ 6. It takes the same force to move a heavy box and a light box up the same inclined plane.

_____ 7. Complex means "having many parts."

_____ 8. A can opener is an example of a complex machine.

Applying Strategies: Summarize

Use complete sentences to answer question 9. (2 points)

9. Name a complex machine. Then write a sentence that summarizes the simple machines that work together in this complex machine.

_____

_____

_____

_____

Using the Effort and Load Equation

The equation shows how the effort, load, and fulcrum are related in a lever.

effort × distance from fulcrum = load × distance from fulcrum

Use the formula to complete the chart.

Effort	×	Distance	=	Load	×	Distance
5	×		=	10	×	2
6	×	4	=	8	×	
15	×	3	=		×	5
20	×		=	10	×	8
9	×	4	=	6	×	
6	×	7	=		×	21
	×	25	=	5	×	10
	×	2	=	5	×	6

Notes for Home: Your child learned how to use an equation to find an unknown value.

Home Activity: Have your child solve simple equations such as 7 + x = 10 or x − 6 = 9.

Notes

Dear Family,

Your child is learning how simple machines help do work. In the science chapter Simple Machines, our class has learned about levers, wheels and axles, pulleys, inclined planes, wedges, and screws. The children have also learned that simple machines can be put together to make complex machines.

In addition to learning about simple machines, the children have also learned many new vocabulary words. Help your child to make these words a part of his or her own vocabulary by using them when you talk together about simple machines.

lever
fulcrum
load
effort
wheel and axle
pulley
inclined plane
wedge
screw

The following pages include activities that you and your child can do together. By participating in your child's education, you will help to bring the learning home.

Family Science Activity

Exploring Levers

Materials

- 12-inch ruler
- wooden pencil (with flat sides)
- pennies
- paper
- pencil

Steps

1. Place the pencil under the ruler at the 4-inch mark to make a lever.

2. Have your child place ten pennies at the end of the ruler, by the 1-inch mark.
   Add pennies to the opposite side of the ruler, near the 12-inch mark until the ten pennies are lifted off the table. Have your child write down the number of pennies.

3. Repeat the activity but this time place the pencil under the ruler at the 8-inch mark.

4. Compare the results from each experiment with your child.

5. Discuss with your child how more pennies were needed to lift the ten pennies when the pencil was at the 8-inch mark. This is because the fulcrum (pencil) was placed further away from the object being moved. Encourage your child to explain, in his or her own words, how a lever works.

Workbook

Simple Machines

Look at the pictures.
Draw a line from the name of the simple machine to the picture that shows the simple machine.

wheel and axle

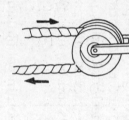

lever

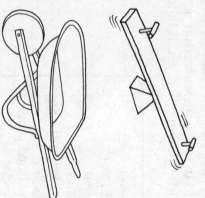

wedge

pulley

Complex Machines

Look at the picture.
Circle the simple machines you see in the picture.
Write the names of the simple machines on the lines.

_____

_____

Fun Fact

No one is sure what the first simple machine was, but some people think that it might have been a lever. People probably used large sticks to move heavy rocks that they could not lift up. They made a simple machine from the objects around them.

Name _____

The Personal Vocabulary Journal below contains vocabulary words and sentences using the words. Use clues from the sentences to help you predict the definition of the words. Check and, if necessary, revise your predictions as you read the chapter.

Personal Vocabulary Journal		
Word	**Word in Sentence**	**Predicted Definition**
axis	Earth rotates on its **axis,** which extends from pole to pole.	
rotation	The **rotation** of Earth every 24 hours results in night and day.	
revolution	Earth makes one **revolution** around the Sun every 365 days.	
orbit	Earth **orbits** around the Sun.	
ellipse	The orbits of planets are shaped like **ellipses.**	
lunar eclipse	During a **lunar eclipse,** a shadow seems to make the Moon disappear.	
solar eclipse	During a **solar eclipse,** the Moon is between Earth and the Sun.	
constellation	The little dipper makes up much of the **constellation** Ursa Minor.	

Notes for Home: Your child learned the vocabulary terms for Chapter 17.
Home Activity: Have your child use illustrations from his or her textbook to provide examples that help define the vocabulary words. Use the words as you talk about the solar system.

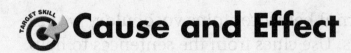

Cause and Effect

Read the paragraph below explaining why there are tides.

Why Are There Tides?

The tide goes in and the tide goes out. What causes this? The Moon revolves around Earth. As it does, the Moon's gravity pulls on Earth's surface water. The water facing the Moon swells toward the Moon. At the same time, Earth is spinning. On the other side of Earth, the spinning causes the water to swell. On these two sides, water is at high tide.

The levels of the tides are different every day and from place to place. Sometimes the Sun and the Moon are lined up. Then very high tides and very low tides happen. At other times, the difference in the tides is not so great.

Apply It!

Answer the questions on the next page about causes and effects.

1. How does the Moon affect Earth's water?

   _____

   _____

   _____

2. How does the spinning of Earth affect Earth's water?

   _____

   _____

   _____

3. What causes very high and very low tides?

   _____

   _____

   _____

4. Why do some areas have low tides when others have high tide?

   _____

   _____

   _____

Notes for Home: Your child learned how to summarize information.
Home Activity: Help your child find pictures of a place at high tide and at low tide. Talk about the differences in appearance of the place during the different tides.

Notes

Lesson 1: How does Earth move?

Before You Read Lesson 1

Read each statement below. Place a check mark in the circle to indicate whether you agree or disagree with the statement.

		Agree	Disagree
1.	All things on Earth move at the same speed.	○	○
2.	Earth takes exactly 24 hours to make a full turn around its axis.	○	○
3.	Earth rotates from west to east.	○	○
4.	The shape of Earth's orbit is circular.	○	○

After You Read Lesson 1

Reread each statement above. If the lesson supports your choice, place a check mark in the *Correct* circle. Then explain how the text supports your choice. If the lesson does not support your choice, place a check mark in the *Incorrect* circle. Then explain why your choice is wrong.

		Correct	Incorrect
1.	_____	○	○
	_____		
2.	_____	○	○
	_____		
3.	_____	○	○
	_____		
4.	_____	○	○
	_____		

Notes for Home: Your child has completed a pre/post inventory of key concepts in the lesson.
Home Activity: Using a small and a large ball, have your child demonstrate how Earth rotates on its axis and how it revolves around the Sun.

Reviewing Terms: Matching

Match each description with the correct word. Write the letter on the line next to each description.

_____ 1. an imaginary pole that goes through Earth's center

_____ 2. the spinning of Earth around its axis

_____ 3. the movement of one object around another

_____ 4. the path Earth takes around the Sun

_____ 5. a circle that is stretched in opposite directions

a. orbit

b. axis

c. rotation

d. revolution

e. ellipse

Reviewing Concepts: Sentence Completion

Complete each sentence with the correct word.

_____ 6. It takes 23 hours and 56 minutes for Earth to complete one _____. (revolution, rotation)

_____ 7. When a place on Earth is turned away from the Sun, it is _____ at that spot. (day, night)

_____ 8. The force of _____ keeps Earth in its orbit. (friction, gravity)

Applying Strategies: Cause and Effect

Use a complete sentence to answer question 9. (2 points)

9. What is the cause of the change in the size and position of shadows during the day?

_____

_____

_____

_____

Lesson 2: What patterns can you see in the sky?

Before You Read Lesson 2

Read each statement below. Place a check mark in the circle to indicate whether you agree or disagree with the statement.

	Agree	Disagree
1. The Moon produces its own light.	○	○
2. It takes the Moon about 1 month to complete a revolution around Earth.	○	○
3. A new Moon is not visible.	○	○
4. A solar eclipse is visible from anywhere on Earth.	○	○

After You Read Lesson 2

Reread each statement above. If the lesson supports your choice, place a check mark in the *Correct* circle. Then explain how the text supports your choice. If the lesson does not support your choice, place a check mark in the *Incorrect* circle. Then explain why your choice is wrong.

	Correct	Incorrect
1. _____	○	○
_____		
2. _____	○	○
_____		
3. _____	○	○
_____		
4. _____	○	○
_____		

Notes for Home: Your child has completed a pre/post inventory of key concepts in the lesson.
Home Activity: Using a flashlight and three balls, help your child model solar and lunar eclipses. Discuss how they are alike and different.

Reviewing Terms: Sentence Completion

Complete each sentence with the correct word.

_____ 1. When one object in space gets between the Sun and another object, a(n) _____ occurs. (eclipse, constellation)

_____ 2. A _____ eclipse happens when the Moon passes through Earth's shadow. (solar, lunar)

_____ 3. When the Moon casts a shadow on Earth, a _____ eclipse occurs. (solar, lunar)

_____ 4. Patterns of stars in the sky are called _____. (phases, constellations)

Reviewing Concepts: True or False

Write **T** (True) or **F** (False) on the line before each statement.

_____ 5. The Moon produces its own light.

_____ 6. During a full Moon, the Moon looks like a full circle.

_____ 7. It is not safe to look directly at the Sun during an eclipse.

_____ 8. Stars appear to move due to Earth's rotation.

Applying Strategies: Decimals

9. Total solar eclipses can last up to 7.5 minutes. Write two mixed numbers that are equal to 7.5. (2 points)

Comparing Average Temperatures

The table below shows the average temperature for 4 months for a city in the Northern Hemisphere (Dublin, Ireland), in the Southern Hemisphere (Sydney, Australia), and close to the equator (Honolulu, Hawaii).

Average Temperature by Month (°Celsius)			
Month	Dublin, Ireland	Honolulu, Hawaii	Sydney, Australia
January	4.8°	22.7°	21.8°
April	7.8°	24.3°	17.8°
July	15.0°	26.9°	10.7°
October	9.7°	26.4°	17.0°

Use the data in the table to answer the questions.

1. Find the average (mean) temperature in Dublin, Ireland, for the 4 months.

   _____

2. In which month are the average temperatures for Honolulu, Hawaii, and Sydney, Australia, most alike?

   _____

3. In which month are the average temperatures for Dublin, Ireland, and Sydney, Australia, most different?

   _____

4. What is the range of average temperatures in each city?

   _____

Notes for Home: Your child learned how to use a table of data to answer questions.
Home Activity: Use a newspaper to find and compare the temperatures of a city near you with other cities in the world. Are the temperatures close or very different?

Notes

Dear Family,

Your child is learning about the different ways Earth and the Moon move. In the science chapter Earth's Cycles, our class has learned about the rotation and revolution of Earth. Students have also learned about why the Moon appears to change shape throughout the month.

In addition to learning about solar eclipses, lunar eclipses, and constellations, students have also learned many new vocabulary words. Help your child to make these words a part of his or her own vocabulary by using them when you talk together about Earth's cycles.

> axis
> rotation
> revolution
> orbit
> ellipse
> eclipse
> lunar eclipse
> solar eclipse
> constellation

The following pages include activities that you and your child can do together. By participating in your child's education, you will help to bring the learning home.

Family Science Activity
Exploring Moon Phases

Materials:

- Lamp
- Styrofoam ball
- Pencil

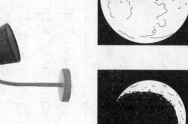

Steps

1. Place the lamp on a table and tell your child that the lamp represents the Sun.

2. Slide the pencil into the Styrofoam ball. Have your child hold the ball in front of himself or herself. Explain that the ball represents the Moon and your child represents Earth.

3. Instruct your child to start by standing in front of the lamp. The ball should be between your child and the lamp. Ask your child how much of the ball appears to be lit. [The ball should not be lit at this time.] Have your child identify this Moon phase. [New Moon]

4. Continue having your child turn around in a circle. Discuss how the Moon's shape appears to change as the Moon revolves around Earth. [Note: Your child may have to duck down when his or her body is between the lamp and the ball.]

Solar and Lunar Eclipses

Draw a picture showing the positions of the Sun, Moon, and Earth during a solar eclipse and a lunar eclipse. Be sure to label your diagrams with the words **Sun**, **Moon**, and **Earth**.

Solar Eclipse	Lunar Eclipse

What causes that?

Using phrases from the box, write the cause of each event.

> Earth's tilted axis
> Moon's revolution
> Earth's revolution
> Earth's rotation

A. Length of Day _____   B. Phases of the Moon _____

C. Changing Seasons _____   D. Length of a Year _____

Fun Fact

During winter in the United States, Earth is actually closer to the Sun than it is during the summer. However, the United States is pointing away from the Sun. The temperatures are colder because there is less direct sunlight.

Workbook

Each of the vocabulary words below is used once to complete the sentences. Choose the term that completes each sentence.

galaxy	universe	solar system	space probe
craters	satellite	astronomy	

1. The study of the Sun, Moon, stars, and other objects in space is _____.

2. The _____ is all of space and everything in it.

3. A _____ is a system of millions to trillions of stars, gases, and dust held together by gravity.

4. A _____ is the large hole that is made when a meteorite crashes into a planet or moon.

5. The _____ includes the Sun, the planets, their moons, and other objects that orbit the Sun.

6. A _____ is an object that orbits another object in space.

7. A _____ is a vehicle that carries cameras and other tools for studying different objects in space.

Notes for Home: Your child learned the vocabulary terms for Chapter 18.
Home Activity: Have your child use the vocabulary terms in sentences. Focus on writing sentences related to our solar system.

Name _____

⊙ Predicting

Read the newspaper article.

Blue Moon

Have you ever heard the expression "once in a blue moon"?
What do people mean when they say that? There are two
definitions of *blue moon*, one more technical than the other. The
most common meaning of *blue moon* is the second full moon in
any calendar month. The average time between full moons is
about 29.5 days, and the average month is 30.5 days. As a result,
two full moons in one month rarely occur. In fact, a blue moon

happens only about once every $2\frac{1}{2}$ years. Blue moons will not

occur in 2006, 2011, 2014, and 2017.

Apply It!

Use the information to answer the questions on the next page.

1. If a blue moon occurs at the end of June 2007, when is another blue moon likely?

   _____

   _____

2. When will blue moons occur between 2010 and 2017?

   _____

   _____

3. On July 2, 2004, a full moon appeared. Did this month have a blue moon?

   _____

   _____

4. When people say "once in a blue moon," they are not actually talking about the blue moon. What do you think they mean by this phrase?

   _____

   _____

Notes for Home: Your child learned how to make predictions.
Home Activity: Help your child predict the day of the next full moon based on the day that the last full moon occurred.

Notes

Lesson 1: What makes up the universe?

Before You Read Lesson 1

Read each statement below. Place a check mark in the circle to indicate whether you agree or disagree with the statement.

	Agree	Disagree
1. Most of the universe is empty space.	◯	◯
2. All galaxies have the same shape.	◯	◯
3. The Moon is part of the solar system.	◯	◯
4. Our Sun is the largest star in the universe.	◯	◯

After You Read Lesson 1

Reread each statement above. If the lesson supports your choice, place a check mark in the *Correct* circle. Then explain how the text supports your choice. If the lesson does not support your choice, place a check mark in the *Incorrect* circle. Then explain why your choice is wrong.

	Correct	Incorrect
1. _____	◯	◯
_____		
2. _____	◯	◯
_____		
3. _____	◯	◯
_____		
4. _____	◯	◯
_____		

Notes for Home: Your child has completed a pre/post inventory of key concepts in the lesson.
Home Activity: Help your child find and read articles about the solar system or universe in newspapers.

Reviewing Terms: Matching

Match each description with the correct word or phrase. Write the letter on the line next to each description.

_____ 1. all of space and everything in it

_____ 2. a system of billions of stars, gases, and dust

_____ 3. the study of the Sun, Moon, stars, and other objects in the sky

_____ 4. the Sun, the planets, their moons, and other objects

a. galaxy

b. solar system

c. universe

d. astronomy

Reviewing Concepts: Sentence Completion

Complete each sentence with the correct word or phrase.

_____ 5. In the solar system, _____ objects revolve around the Sun. (some, all)

_____ 6. Asteroids are _____ than planets. (larger, smaller)

_____ 7. The Sun is a _____. (planet, star)

_____ 8. The largest object in the solar system is _____. (Jupiter, the Sun)

Writing

Use a complete sentence to answer question 9. (2 points)

9. Write a sentence that tells one way that an early civilization used astronomy.

_____

_____

Lesson 2: What are the inner planets?

Before You Read Lesson 2

Read each statement below. Place a check mark in the circle to indicate whether you agree or disagree with the statement.

	Agree	Disagree
1. Earth is the smallest rocky planet in the solar system.	○	○
2. Venus appears as one of the brightest planets in the solar system when viewed from Earth.	○	○
3. Earth is the only planet with an atmosphere.	○	○
4. All planets have at least one moon.	○	○

After You Read Lesson 2

Reread each statement above. If the lesson supports your choice, place a check mark in the *Correct* circle. Then explain how the text supports your choice. If the lesson does not support your choice, place a check mark in the *Incorrect* circle. Then explain why your choice is wrong.

	Correct	Incorrect
1. _____	○	○
_____		
2. _____	○	○
_____		
3. _____	○	○
_____		
4. _____	○	○
_____		

Notes for Home: Your child has completed a pre/post inventory of key concepts in the lesson.
Home Activity: Help your child draw a model of the solar system showing the inner planets in order. Keep the drawing for the next Home Activity.

Reviewing Terms: Matching

Match each description with the correct word or phrase. Write the letter on the line next to each description.

_____ 1. dents shaped like bowls

_____ 2. a vehicle that carries cameras and other tools into space

_____ 3. objects that orbit another object in space

a. space probe

b. satellites

c. craters

Reviewing Concepts: True or False

Write **T** (True) or **F** (False) on the line before each statement.

_____ 4. Mercury has many moons.

_____ 5. Mercury is very hot during the day and very cold at night.

_____ 6. Earth and Venus are two planets that support life.

_____ 7. Moons are held in orbit by the force of gravity.

_____ 8. Mars has many volcanoes on its surface.

Applying Strategies: Decimals and Percentages

9. Dry rocks and dust cover $\frac{4}{5}$ of the surface of Mars. Write a decimal and a percentage that are equivalent to $\frac{4}{5}$. (2 points)

Name _____

Lesson 3: What do we know about Jupiter, Saturn, and Uranus?

Before You Read Lesson 3

Read each statement below. Place a check mark in the circle to indicate whether you agree or disagree with the statement.

	Agree	Disagree
1. Jupiter is made mostly of gases.	○	○
2. Jupiter's moon, Io, is the largest moon in the solar system.	○	○
3. Saturn's rings are made of gases.	○	○
4. Scientists do not know how many moons Uranus has.	○	○

After You Read Lesson 3

Reread each statement above. If the lesson supports your choice, place a check mark in the *Correct* circle. Then explain how the text supports your choice. If the lesson does not support your choice, place a check mark in the *Incorrect* circle. Then explain why your choice is wrong.

	Correct	Incorrect
1. _____	○	○
_____		
2. _____	○	○
_____		
3. _____	○	○
_____		
4. _____	○	○
_____		

Notes for Home: Your child has completed a pre/post inventory of key concepts in the lesson.
Home Activity: Have your child add Jupiter, Saturn, and Uranus to the drawing from the previous Home Activity.

Reviewing Concepts: Sentence Completion

Complete each sentence with the correct word.

_____ 1. _____ is the largest planet in the solar system. (Jupiter, Saturn)

_____ 2. Galileo was the first person to see the moons of _____. (Uranus, Jupiter)

_____ 3. _____ has a weather system called the "Great Red Spot." (Uranus, Jupiter)

_____ 4. _____ is the sixth planet from the Sun. (Saturn, Uranus)

_____ 5. The Voyager space probe explored the rings of _____. (Jupiter, Saturn)

_____ 6. _____ has a moon with an atmosphere. (Jupiter, Saturn)

_____ 7. _____ is a planet that rotates on its side. (Saturn, Uranus)

_____ 8. The seventh planet from the Sun is _____. (Jupiter, Uranus)

Applying Strategies: Standard Notation

9. The diameter of Jupiter is one hundred and forty-two thousand, nine hundred and eighty-four kilometers. Write this number in standard notation. (2 points)

Lesson 4: What do we know about Neptune, Pluto, and beyond?

Before You Read Lesson 4

Read each statement below. Place a check mark in the circle to indicate whether you agree or disagree with the statement.

	Agree	Disagree
1. Neptune's Great Dark Spot is a giant volcano.	○	○
2. Neptune has at least 13 moons.	○	○
3. Pluto is the solar system's smallest planet.	○	○
4. In 2003, astronomers discovered Sedna, a small, icy object orbiting the Sun beyond Pluto.	○	○

After You Read Lesson 4

Reread each statement above. If the lesson supports your choice, place a check mark in the *Correct* circle. Then explain how the text supports your choice. If the lesson does not support your choice, place a check mark in the *Incorrect* circle. Then explain why your choice is wrong.

	Correct	Incorrect
1. _____	○	○
_____		
2. _____	○	○
_____		
3. _____	○	○
_____		
4. _____	○	○
_____		

Notes for Home: Your child has completed a pre-/post-inventory of key concepts in the lesson.
Home Activity: Have your child add Neptune and Pluto to the drawing from the previous Home Activity.

Name _____

Reviewing Concepts: True or False

Write **T** (True) or **F** (False) on the line before each statement.

_____ 1. Neptune is the largest of the gas giants.

_____ 2. Neptune is the eighth planet from the Sun.

_____ 3. Pluto is an inner planet.

_____ 4. Pluto is a gas giant.

_____ 5. Pluto is a planet with one moon.

_____ 6. Pluto's orbit is not at the same angle as the orbits
of other planets.

_____ 7. Sedna and Pluto are both smaller than Earth's Moon.

_____ 8. Sedna is farther from the Sun than Pluto.

Applying Strategies: Predicting

Use complete sentences to answer question 9. (2 points)

9. It takes Pluto 248 years to revolve around the Sun. Predict whether
it takes Sedna more or less time than Pluto to revolve around the
Sun. Write a sentence that explains your prediction.

_____

_____

_____

Workbook

Using Data About Planets

The table below gives the distance in kilometers of each planet from the Sun.

Planet	(Average) Distance from Sun (in kilometers)	Distance (rounded to the nearest million)
Mercury	57,900,000	
Venus	108,200,000	
Earth	149,600,000	
Mars	227,900,000	
Jupiter	778,400,000	
Saturn	1,426,700,000	
Uranus	2,870,970,000	
Neptune	4,498,300,000	
Pluto	5,906,400,000	

Use the table above to complete the items below.

1. Round each distance to the nearest million. Write the rounded distance in the chart.

2. What is the median rounded distance from the Sun? Which planet is that distance from the Sun?

   _____

3. Which planet is about 10 times farther from the Sun than Earth is?

   _____

Notes for Home: Your child learned how to round numbers to the nearest million.
Home Activity: Write large numbers like those in the table above and have your child round each number to the nearest million, ten million, or hundred million.

Notes

Dear Family,

Your child is learning about the planets in the solar system. In the science chapter Inner and Outer Planets, our class has studied the planets and their moons. The children have learned about characteristics of each of the planets. Our class has also learned about space exploration.

In addition to learning about the planets, the children have also learned many new vocabulary words. Help your child to make these words a part of his or her own vocabulary by using them when you talk together about the planets.

> universe
> galaxy
> astronomy
> solar system
> space probe
> craters
> satellite

The following pages include activities that you and your child can do together. By participating in your child's education, you will help to bring the learning home.

Family Science Activity

Planet Mobiles

Materials

- construction paper
- markers
- string
- hanger
- scissors

Steps

1. Look at the planets on page 2 of this sheet.
2. Using the construction paper and markers, draw a paper model of each planet.
3. Poke a small hole in each planet and tie a piece of string through the planet.
4. Then, tie the planets onto the hanger as a mobile. Make sure the planets are in the correct order from the Sun.
5. Use the model to reference the planets as you discuss the planets with your child.

Workbook

Name That Planet

Label each planet in the picture using a word from the word box.

Mars	Earth	Mercury
Venus	Neptune	Saturn
Uranus	Pluto	Jupiter

Sun

Answers, left to right: Mercury, Venus, Earth, Mars, Jupiter, Saturn, Uranus, Neptune, Pluto

Which Planet Am I?

Write the name of the planet for each riddle.

1. I am the closest planet to the Sun. During the day I am very hot, but at night I am very cold. What planet am I? _____

2. I am one of the inner planets. The mineral iron oxide on my surface is like rust. This gave me my nickname, "The Red Planet." What planet am I? _____

3. My rings are made of water, ice, dust, and chunks of rock. Galileo called my rings handles. What planet am I? _____

4. I am one of the outer planets. I am the smallest planet in the solar system. What planet am I? _____

Fun Fact

The Skylab astronauts had an interesting side effect to their travel in space. The astronauts came home 1.5–2.25 inches taller than when they left. This sudden change was caused by zero gravity.

Answers: 1. Mercury, 2. Mars, 3. Saturn, 4. Pluto

Name _____

Each vocabulary word is used in a sentence to give you a clue to its meaning. Read each sentence, and then write the letter of the correct definition on the line.

Definition	Word	Definition
_____	1. **technology:** Technology changes the way we live, work, and communicate.	**a** Thin manufactured tubes that allow light to pass through them.
_____	2. **optical fibers:** Doctors use cameras with optical fibers to see inside the body.	**b** Communications that are done electronically.
_____	3. **communication:** Letters and email are both forms of communication.	**c** A device that carries people and things from place to place.
_____	4. **telecommunications:** A radio uses telecommunications to send signals.	**d** The knowledge, processes, and products we use to change nature.
_____	5. **vehicle:** Airplanes and boats are examples of vehicles.	**e** The process of sending any type of message from one place to another.

Notes for Home: Your child learned the vocabulary terms for Chapter 19.
Home Activity: Help your child take an inventory of your home to find examples of items that illustrate the vocabulary words.

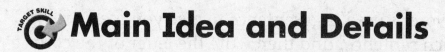
Main Idea and Details

Read the paragraph about ultrasound technology.

"Seeing" with Sound Waves

Doctors make use of ultrasound technology. They use ultrasound to "see" inside the body. During an ultrasound scan, sound waves are sent through the body. The returning sound waves are translated into pictures that specialists read to help make medical diagnoses. Using ultrasound technology, doctors can see into the body without surgery. Doctors may be able to avoid more invasive diagnostic techniques by using ultrasound technology.

Apply It!

Use the graphic organizer on the next page to record details and the main idea from the paragraph.

Main Idea

Detail	Detail

Detail	Detail

Notes for Home: Your child learned how to identify the details and main idea of a paragraph.
Home Activity: Have your child identify the main idea and details in a newspaper or magazine article.

Notes

Lesson 1: How does technology affect our lives?

Before You Read Lesson 1

Read each statement below. Place a check mark in the circle to indicate whether you agree or disagree with the statement.

	Agree	Disagree
1. Technology both solves and creates problems.	○	○
2. Plastic is a natural material.	○	○
3. Fertilizers are good for the environment.	○	○
4. Too much exposure to X-rays can be harmful.	○	○

After You Read Lesson 1

Reread each statement above. If the lesson supports your choice, place a check mark in the *Correct* circle. Then explain how the text supports your choice. If the lesson does not support your choice, place a check mark in the *Incorrect* circle. Then explain why your choice is wrong.

	Correct	Incorrect
1. _____	○	○
_____		
2. _____	○	○
_____		
3. _____	○	○
_____		
4. _____	○	○
_____		

Notes for Home: Your child has completed a pre/post inventory of key concepts in the lesson.
Home Activity: Brainstorm a list of technological innovations. Discuss with your child the possible benefits and drawbacks of each technology.

Reviewing Terms: Sentence Completion

Complete each sentence with the correct word or phrase.

_____ 1. Knowledge, processes, and products used by people to solve problems are _____. (technology, materials)

_____ 2. Thin tubes that allow light to pass are called _____. (X-rays, optical fibers)

Reviewing Concepts: True or False

Write **T** (True) or **F** (False) on the line before each statement.

_____ 3. Technology has only good effects.

_____ 4. Technology can lead to new inventions.

_____ 5. Plastic is a material made with iron ore.

_____ 6. An object that decomposes will become a part of Earth again.

_____ 7. Lasers are a technology used in medicine.

_____ 8. X-rays are the only technology used to view inside the body.

Applying Strategies: Main Idea and Details

Use complete sentences to answer question 9. (2 points)

9. Write two details that support the main idea.

   Main Idea: Technology can be used to help keep us healthy.

   Detail: _____

   _____

   Detail: _____

   _____

Name _____

Think, Read, Learn

Use with pages 556–559.

Lesson 2: How has technology changed communication and transportation?

Before You Read Lesson 2

Read each statement below. Place a check mark in the circle to indicate whether you agree or disagree with the statement.

	Agree	Disagree
1. Clapping is a form of communicating.	○	○
2. People began communicating about 6,000 years ago.	○	○
3. *Telecommunication* means "to communicate by telephone."	○	○
4. An elevator is a type of vehicle.	○	○

After You Read Lesson 2

Reread each statement above. If the lesson supports your choice, place a check mark in the *Correct* circle. Then explain how the text supports your choice. If the lesson does not support your choice, place a check mark in the *Incorrect* circle. Then explain why your choice is wrong.

	Correct	Incorrect
1. _____ _____	○	○
2. _____ _____	○	○
3. _____ _____	○	○
4. _____ _____	○	○

 Notes for Home: Your child has completed a pre/post inventory of key concepts in the lesson.
Home Activity: Help your child develop a list of ways that people around the world communicate with one another. Identify the forms of communication that you and your family use most often.

© Pearson Education, Inc.

Workbook

Think, Read, Learn **179**

Reviewing Terms: Matching

Match each description with the correct word. Write the letter on the line next to each description.

_____ 1. the process of sending a message from one place to another

_____ 2. sending a message electronically

_____ 3. something that carries people and goods

a. vehicle

b. communication

c. telecommunications

Reviewing Concepts: Sentence Completion

Complete each sentence with the correct word or phrase.

_____ 4. Communication can take _____. (one form, many forms)

_____ 5. Electricity has made communication between distant locations _____. (faster, slower)

_____ 6. Airplanes and trains are forms of _____. (communication, transportation)

_____ 7. Air bags and seatbelts are technology designed to make transportation _____. (faster, safer)

_____ 8. Vehicles _____ changed over time. (have, have not)

Writing

Use a complete sentence to answer question 9. (2 points)

9. Write a sentence that describes how computers are a part of modern transportation systems.

_____

_____

_____

Scale Drawings

A scale drawing uses a ratio to show how distances on the drawing are related to the actual distances. Look at the scale drawing of a baseball diamond.

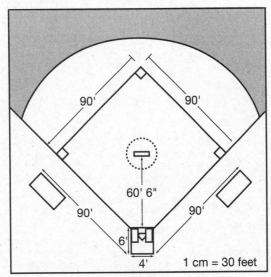

Use the scale drawing to answer each question.

1. What is the scale of the drawing?

    _____

2. How many centimeters are between home plate and third base in the drawing?

    _____

3. What is the actual distance between home plate and third base?

    _____

4. About how far does the pitcher stand from home plate?

    _____

5. A coaches box is 15 feet from the line between third base and home plate. How far from the line on the drawing would you draw the coaches box?

    _____

Notes for Home: Your child learned how to answer questions about a scale drawing.
Home Activity: Look at a map with your child. Use the scale of the map to find the actual distances between different locations on the map.

Notes

Dear Family,

In the science chapter Effects of Technology, our class has learned about how technology has affected our daily lives. In particular, our class has learned how technology is used in communication systems and transportation systems.

In addition to learning how these systems have changed over time, students have also learned many new vocabulary words. Help your child to make these words a part of his or her own vocabulary by using them when you talk together about technology.

technology
optical fibers
communication
telecommunications
vehicle

The following pages include activities that you and your child can do together. By participating in your child's education, you will help to bring the learning home.

© Pearson Education, Inc.

Family Science Activity

Exploring Communication Technology

Materials:

- Paper
- Pencils

Steps

1. For one evening, prohibit all family members from using modern communication devices, such as televisions, telephones, and computers.

2. As you do so, encourage all family members to keep a list of devices they find themselves needing or wanting to use.

3. As a family, discuss the challenges of being unable to use these modern communication devices to receive and give information. Discuss how life is different now compared to times when such technological devices were not available.

4. With your child, brainstorm how technology might change communication in the next ten to twenty years.

Workbook

Vocabulary Practice

Unscramble the vocabulary words on the left.
Match the vocabulary words to their definitions on the right.

(emnstaeocmtulociin) _____

(cnloetyhogn) _____

(tcploia eibfr) _____

(hvceeli) _____

(nomiuctmcinao) _____

the part of a transportation system that carries people and goods

the process of sending any type of message from one place to another

the knowledge, processes, and products that we use to solve problems and make our work easier

communications that are done electronically

very thin tubes that allow light to pass through them

Technology and Transportation

Number the kinds of transportation from the earliest to the most recent.

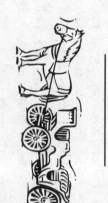

Fun Fact

There are about 127 million cars in America today. If they were lined up bumper-to-bumper, they could wrap around Earth eighteen times.

Answers: 3, 2, 4, 1, 5

Name _____

How are living things classified?

The world is filled with more than one million kinds of organisms. Scientists use a classification system to identify, compare, and study living things. The largest classification group is a kingdom. Today, many scientists classify organisms into six kingdoms. All organisms in a group are like each other in some way.

Kingdoms of Living Things

One-Celled Organisms

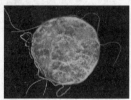

Ancient Bacteria

True Bacteria

Protists

Many-Celled Organisms

Fungi

Plants

Animals

Answer these questions about the pictures above.

1. How many kingdoms are made of one-celled organisms?

   _____

2. Are fungi one-celled or many-celled organisms?

   _____

3. How are protists different from plants?

   _____

   _____

4. How are animals and fungi the same?

   _____

Which animals have backbones?

The animal kingdom is divided into two main groups: vertebrates and invertebrates. Vertebrates have backbones. They are divided into the five groups shown below.

Vertebrates

Mammals   Birds   Reptiles

Amphibians   Fish

Answer these questions about the pictures above.

1. Which group lives only in the water?

   _____

2. Which group is covered with hair or fur?

   _____

3. What are birds covered with?

   _____

4. Which two groups are covered with scales?

   _____

What is in a leaf cell?

Photosynthesis is the process in which plants change carbon dioxide, water, and nutrients into oxygen, sugars, and other foods. Photosynthesis takes place in the chloroplasts of leaf cells. Stoma are tiny openings that are found on the underside of most leaves. Stoma let water and gases into and out of the leaf. The cell membrane lets water, food, and gases pass into and out of the cell.

Parts of a Leaf Cell

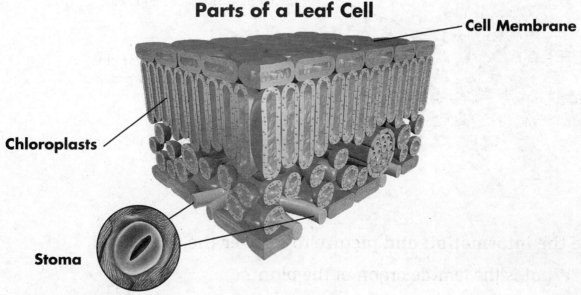

Cell Membrane

Chloroplasts

Stoma

Answer these questions about leaf cells.

1. What are three parts of a leaf cell as shown in the diagram?

    _____

2. Where are stoma found on most leaves?

    _____

3. How do plants make their own food? What is this process called?

    _____

    _____

4. Where does photosynthesis take place?

    _____

5. What is the cell membrane's job?

    _____

Name _____

What is pollination and fertilization?

The movement of pollen from stamen to pistil is called pollination. The ovary is the part of the plant that has egg cells. Fertilization happens when sperm cells from pollen combine with egg cells.

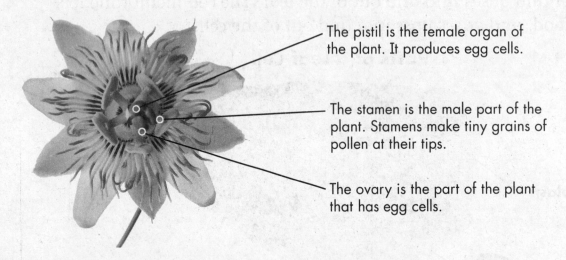

The pistil is the female organ of the plant. It produces egg cells.

The stamen is the male part of the plant. Stamens make tiny grains of pollen at their tips.

The ovary is the part of the plant that has egg cells.

Use the information and picture to answer the questions.

1. What is the female organ of the plant?

   _____

2. What is the male part of the plant?

   _____

3. What is pollination?

   _____

4. What happens when sperm cells from pollen combine with egg cells?

   _____

What do animals eat in their ecosystems?

The Sonoran Desert is an ecosystem. Some animals are herbivores, some are carnivores, and some are omnivores. They form a food web that helps keep the ecosystem balanced.

Consumers of the Sonoran Desert

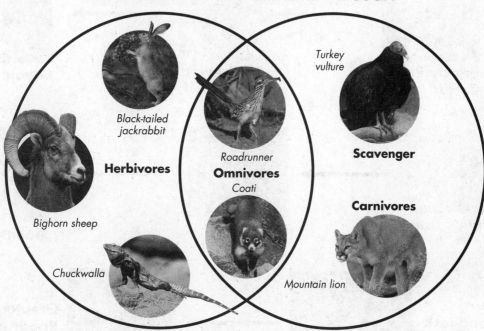

Black-tailed jackrabbit

Herbivores

Bighorn sheep

Chuckwalla

Roadrunner

Omnivores

Coati

Turkey vulture

Scavenger

Carnivores

Mountain lion

Answer these questions about the pictures above.

1. Which animals in the picture eat plants?

   _____

   _____

2. What kind of consumer is a mountain lion?

   _____

3. Why are the omnivores in the middle of the picture?

   _____

4. How is the turkey vulture different from the mountain lion? What kinds of food does the turkey vulture eat?

   _____

   _____

Name _____

What is a food web?

An ecosystem has many food chains. A system of overlapping food chains is called a food web.

A Food Web

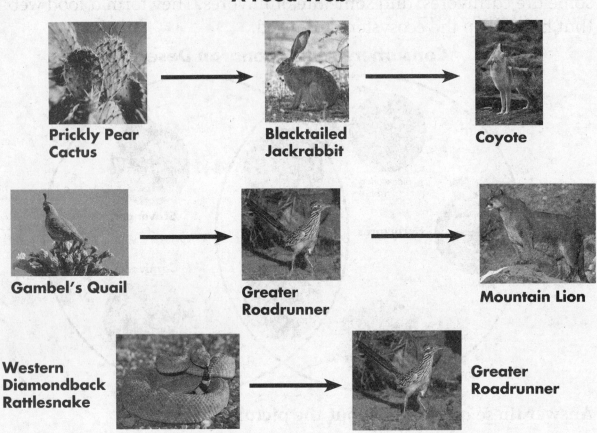

Answer these questions about the food web pictured above.

1. Which animal eats the prickly pear cactus?

   _____

2. What does a greater roadrunner eat?

   _____

3. How is the greater roadrunner both a predator and prey?

   _____

   _____

Name _____

How are ecosystems balanced?

All living things depend on one another and their environments to live and grow. All plants and animals need food, water, living space, shelter, light, and air to be healthy. Interactions among living and nonliving things help maintain balance in ecosystems.

Plants and Animals of the Great Smoky Mountains

Answer these questions about the pictures above.

1. What does a chipmunk need to be healthy?

   _____

   _____

2. What does a raccoon depend on to live and grow?

   _____

   _____

3. When are plants and animals in an ecosystem healthy?

   _____

4. What helps to maintain balance in an ecosystem?

   _____

   _____

How do environments change?

The new lake has no living things. But rivers carry nutrients into the lake.

Then small plants can grow. Insects and herbivores enter the ecosystem.

The lake community has many living things, and the lake slowly fills with soil and fallen leaves. The lake slowly becomes a marsh.

After many years, the marsh dries up. The marsh then gradually becomes a forest.

Use the pictures and information to answer the questions.

1. What is the lake like at first?

   _____

2. What happens after organisms add nutrients to the lake?

   _____

   _____

3. Why are herbivores some of the first animals to enter the ecosystem?

   _____

4. What happens after the marsh dries up?

   _____

Workbook

How do your lungs work?

Your body needs a constant supply of oxygen. Air enters through your nose and mouth. It passes through several organs on its way to your lungs.

The Lungs

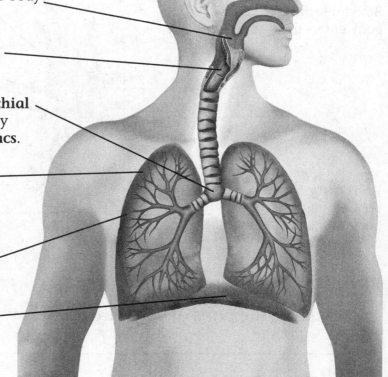

Air moves from outside your body into your mouth and nose.

The **trachea** leads from the **pharynx** toward the lungs.

The trachea splits into two **bronchial tubes**. These tubes divide into tiny branches which lead to the **air sacs**.

The smallest branches lead to tiny air sacs. Each air sac has tiny **blood vessels** around it.

The **lungs** are the main organ of the respiratory system.

The **diaphragm** is the main muscle involved in breathing.

Answer these questions.

1. What organs does air pass through to get from your mouth to your lungs?

   _____

2. What does the trachea do?

   _____

   _____

3. What is wrapped around each air sac?

   _____

4. How is the diaphragm important?

   _____

How does your heart work?

Your circulatory system includes your heart, blood vessels, and blood. Your heart is a pump that works to move blood through your body. The blood brings oxygen to your body's cells.

The Heart

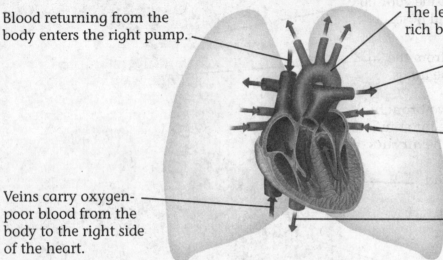

Blood returning from the body enters the right pump.

The left pump moves oxygen-rich blood into the body.

The right pump sends blood to the lungs.

Oxygen-rich blood from the lungs enters the left pump.

Veins carry oxygen-poor blood from the body to the right side of the heart.

Arteries carry oxygen-rich blood from the left side of the heart to the body.

Please answer the questions.

1. What are the parts of your circulatory system?

   _____

2. What is the job of your heart?

   _____

3. What does the right pump of your heart do?

   _____

4. What does the left pump of your heart do?

   _____

5. Which blood vessels carry oxygen-rich blood from the heart to the body?

   _____

6. Which blood vessels carry oxygen-poor blood from the body to the heart?

   _____

How does the water cycle work?

The water cycle is the process of water moving from Earth's surface to the atmosphere and back again.

The Water Cycle

Condensation
When moist air rises, it cools. The water vapor in it condenses in the atmosphere. These tiny droplets of liquid water form clouds and fog.

Precipitation
Depending on air temperatures and wind conditions, the water may fall as rain, snow, or hail. If the air temperature in or below the cloud is above freezing, the water vapor will condense and fall as rain. If the air temperature is below freezing, water falls as snow, sleet, or hail. Most precipitaion falls on oceans.

Evaporation
Water is stored in lakes, oceans, glaciers, marshes, soil, and spaces in rock. It evaporates in the Sun's warmth. Some water vapor also comes from the leaves of plants.

Storage
The water from precipitation over land sinks into soil and underground pores in rock. Some water runs off the land into streams, rivers, and lakes. Most of it falls, flows, or seeps into the ocean.

Answer these questions.

1. Where is water stored on Earth?

   _____

2. What causes water to evaporate?

   _____

3. What forms clouds and fog?

   _____

4. What is precipitation?

   _____

5. What are the different forms of precipitation?

   _____

Name _____

What do we use to measure weather?

Meteorologists use the tools shown below to study weather conditions.

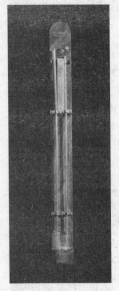

A **barometer** measures air pressure in units called millibars (mb).

A **wind vane** shows the direction from which the wind is blowing. The pointer on the wind vane points into the wind.

An **anemometer** measures wind speed.

A **hygrometer** measures humidity.

Please answer the following questions.

1. What does a wind vane show?

   _____

2. Which tool measures wind speed?

   _____

3. What does a barometer measure?

   _____

4. Which tool measures humidity?

   _____

Workbook

Name _____

What are hurricanes?

A hurricane can cause changes to many of Earth's systems. In many hurricanes, water causes the worst damage. The winds from a hurricane push water in front of the hurricane. This rise in sea level is called a storm surge. The storm surge can cause flooding. The thunderstorms from a hurricane can cause tornadoes on land. Tornadoes can break trees and flatten buildings.

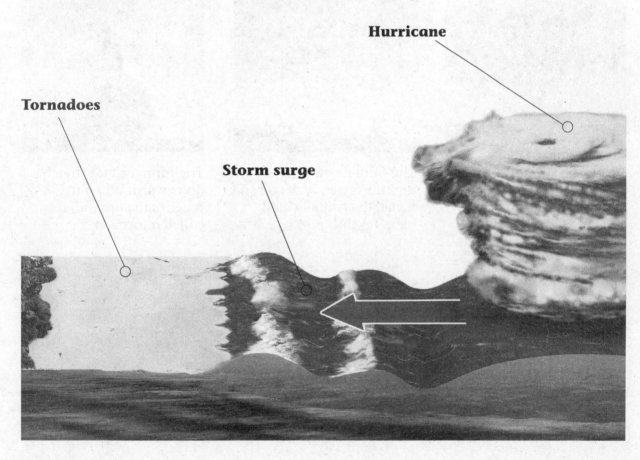

Hurricane

Tornadoes

Storm surge

Answer these questions about hurricanes.

1. What causes the worst damage in hurricanes?

   _____

2. What is a storm surge?

   _____

3. What can a storm surge cause?

   _____

Name _____

How do tornadoes form?

A tornado is a spinning column of air that comes out of a thunderstorm. The pictures below show how a tornado forms.

Inside the spinning storm is a smaller column of air shaped like a funnel.

The funnel gets longer and narrower. As it spins faster, the funnel cloud picks up things in its path.

The funnel cloud stretches downward. When it touches the ground, it is called a tornado.

Answer these questions about tornadoes.

1. What is a tornado?

_____

2. Where does a tornado come from?

_____

3. What happens as the funnel cloud spins faster?

_____

4. When is the funnel cloud called a tornado?

_____

Name _____

How can you identify a mineral?

Rocks are made of minerals. Scientists identify minerals by testing their physical properties such as color, luster, streak, and hardness. Scientists test a mineral's hardness by finding out how easily it can be scratched. The Mohs Scale ranks minerals from 1 to 10, the higher the number, the harder the mineral.

Looking at Minerals

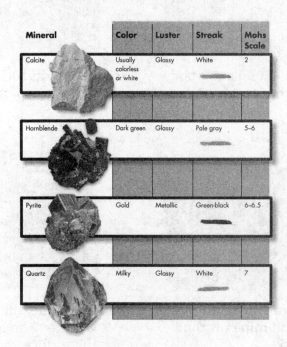

Mineral		Color	Luster	Streak	Mohs Scale
Calcite		Usually colorless or white	Glassy	White	2
Hornblende		Dark green	Glassy	Pale gray	5–6
Pyrite		Gold	Metallic	Green-black	6–6.5
Quartz		Milky	Glassy	White	7

Answer these questions about the minerals in the chart above.

1. Which mineral has a dark green color?

   _____

2. Which mineral is the hardest?

   _____

3. Which mineral has a metallic luster?

   _____

4. Which minerals have a white streak?

   _____

5. Which mineral has a hardness of 5–6 on the Mohs Scale?

   _____

How do fossils form?

Each picture shows a stage in how fossils are formed.

1. After an animal dies, its soft body parts decay. Its hard body parts are left.

2. Sediments such as sand or mud settle on top of the remains.

3. More layers form. The remains are replaced with minerals that harden into rock.

4. Over time, the rock layers weather. The fossil appears at the surface.

Answer these questions about how fossils are formed.

1. After an animal dies, which parts decay?

_____

2. Which parts are left after an animal dies?

_____

3. What settles on top of the remains?

_____

4. The remains are replaced with minerals in the sediment. What happens to these minerals?

_____

Name _____

What are weathering, erosion, and deposition?

In weathering, large rocks are broken down into smaller and smaller pieces. They gradually become soil and sand. Water, ice, gravity, and wind work together to move weathered materials. This is called erosion. Erosion can wear away landforms. Pieces of rock and soil are carried from one place and then deposited at another place by wind and water. This is called deposition.

Answer these questions about weathering, erosion, and deposition.

1. How are weathered materials moved?

   _____

2. Over time, what will the river do to the land?

   _____

3. What happens during deposition?

   _____

   _____

© Pearson Education, Inc.

How do volcanoes form?

Before a volcano forms, things happen deep underground. Hot rock is partly melted into liquid called magma. Gas forces the magma upward. A volcano forms at a weak spot in Earth's crust where magma reaches the surface. When magna flows out of the volcano, it is called lava. Rock, ash, and gas come out of other openings called vents.

A Volcano Erupts

Answer these questions about volcanoes.

1. What is magma?

   _____

2. What makes magma come out of a volcano?

   _____

3. Where do volcanoes form?

   _____

4. What is magma called when it flows out of a volcano?

   _____

5. Which part of a volcano sends out rock, gas, and ash?

   _____

Name _____

What are the different layers of soil?

The top layer of soil is called topsoil. Subsoil, near the surface, is made up mostly of small rocks. The topsoil and subsoil contain air, minerals, and decaying animal and plant matter. Bedrock is mostly solid rock.

Layers of Soil

Topsoil —

Subsoil —

Bedrock —

Answer these questions about the different layers of soil.

1. Which layer of soil is in the middle?

   _____

2. Which layer of soil is mostly made of solid rock?

   _____

3. What do topsoil and subsoil contain?

   _____

4. How is subsoil different from bedrock?

   _____

   _____

   _____

What is recycling?

Recycling is using materials again instead of throwing them away. A recycling symbol on an object shows that it can be recycled.

Paper can be recycled into new paper.

Some plastics are melted, shredded, formed, and recycled into T-shirts, quilted jackets, and sleeping bags.

Old tires can be used in construction, to build fences, make crash cushions, and make equipment for sports and playgrounds.

Answer these questions about recycling.

1. What is recycling?

   _____

2. If you have an empty soda can with a recycling symbol on it, should you throw the can away? Explain.

   _____

3. What must happen to plastic before it is recycled into a T-shirt?

   _____

4. Which material can be recycled and used to build fences?

   _____

What are the three states of matter?

The three states of matter are solid, liquid, and gas. A solid has a definite shape. It usually takes up a definite amount of space. A liquid also takes up a definite amount of space, but it takes the shape of any container into which you pour it. A gas expands to fill the container it is in.

Solid particles are packed tightly together.

Liquid particles are close to each other, but they are not held tightly together.

Gas particles are far apart.

Answer these questions about the three states of matter.

1. Which state of matter has its particles packed tightly together?

   _____

2. Which state of matter has particles that are far apart?

   _____

3. How are liquids and solids different?

   _____

4. How are liquids and gases the same?

   _____

What is a chemical change?

A chemical change produces a completely different kind of matter. In a chemical change, particles of one substance are changed in some way to form particles of a new substance with different properties. The new substance may be a different color. It may have a different smell or temperature. Many chemical changes give off heat.

Chemical Changes

Rust forms slowly as oxygen from the air combines with the iron in the gear.

Tarnish results from a chemical change when certain metals, such as silver, react with air.

Burning wood reacts very quickly with oxygen in the air. The new substances formed by this change are ashes, carbon dioxide gas, and water vapor.

Answer these questions about chemical changes.

1. What happens in a chemical change?

   _____

   _____

2. How did the silver bell become tarnished?

   _____

3. What chemical change resulted when iron combined with oxygen in the air?

   _____

4. Which of the chemical changes pictured gave off heat?

   _____

© Pearson Education, Inc.

How does heat move?

Heat can move in several ways. Conduction is the transfer of heat from one thing touching another thing. Heat moves through some materials easily. These materials are called conductors. But heat does not move easily through materials called insulators.

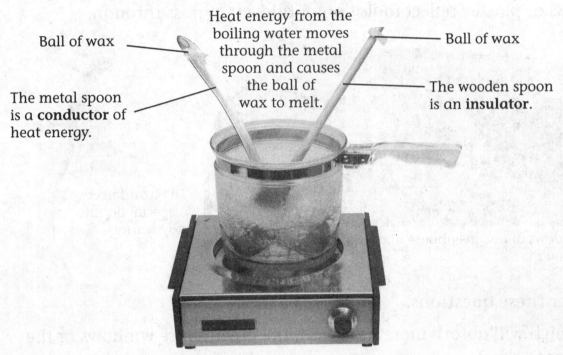

Ball of wax

Heat energy from the boiling water moves through the metal spoon and causes the ball of wax to melt.

Ball of wax

The metal spoon is a **conductor** of heat energy.

The wooden spoon is an **insulator**.

Answer these questions about the picture above.

1. Is the metal spoon or the wooden spoon a conductor?

   _____

2. Which spoon will have a hot handle?

   _____

3. Which spoon will have a cool handle?

   _____

4. Why is the wax melting on the metal spoon?

   _____

Write the answer to this question on the line.

5. What is conduction?

   _____

What is radiation?

Radiation is energy. Radiation gives warmth. You feel radiation standing in the sunlight. Radiation can travel through empty space. This is how the Sun's energy travels to Earth. It can also travel through matter. Dark-colored surfaces absorb radiation. Clear materials, such as glass or plastic, reflect radiation or allow it to pass through.

The windows of the greenhouse allow radiation to pass through.

The lizard needs a special light to stay warm.

Answer these questions.

1. Which will absorb more radiation, the greenhouse windows or the lizard's skin?

   _____

2. What will the temperature be like inside the greenhouse because of the glass windows?

   _____

3. How will dark-colored skin on the lizard help it stay warm?

   _____

4. How does energy move from the Sun to Earth?

   _____

5. What parts of your home let radiation in? Which parts absorb radiation?

   _____

   _____

What are magnetic fields?

All magnets have two poles, a north-seeking pole and a south-seeking pole. Opposite charges attract each other. Charges that are the same repel each other.

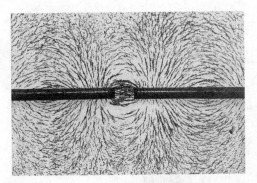

A

The iron filings show that the magnets are pulling toward each other.

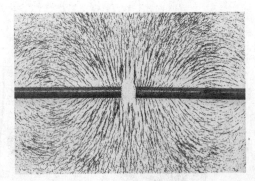

B

The iron filings show that the magnets are pushing away from each other.

Please answer these questions.

1. Which picture shows two magnets that attract each other?

   _____

2. Which picture shows two north-seeking poles pointing at each other?

   _____

3. Does the north-seeking pole of one magnet attract or repel a south-seeking pole of another magnet?

   _____

4. What are the two poles facing each other in picture A?

   _____

5. What will happen to picture B if you turn one of the bar magnets around?

   _____

   _____

Name _____

How do electric charges flow?

An electric current is an electric charge that moves from one place to another. A circuit is a loop of moving electricity. The electricity moves through the circuit. There are different kinds of circuits.

In a **series circuit**, electrical current can only flow in one path. When the power is on, the electric charge flows in one direction around one loop. If one bulb burns out, it opens the circuit. The electric charge will stop flowing through the circuit. The other bulbs will not get any electrical current.

In a **parallel circuit**, electrical current flows in two or more paths. There are different paths for the electric charge to flow through. A break in one part of the circuit does not stop the electrical current from flowing.

Answer these questions about the pictures above.

1. Which circuit has only one path for the electrical current?

   _____

2. Which circuit has two or more paths for electrical current?

   _____

3. What happens to the electric charge if a bulb burns out in a series circuit?

   _____

4. What happens to the electrical current if there is a break in a parallel circuit?

   _____

5. Which kind of circuit is better for wiring a home or school? Why?

   _____

   _____

How does sound travel?

Gases, liquids, and solids are mediums that sound can travel through. Sound travels fastest when the particles in a medium are very close together. It travels slowest when the particles in a medium are far apart.

How Sound Travels

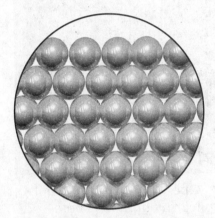  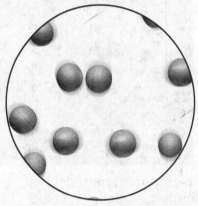

In a **solid**, particles are very close together. Sound travels fastest through solids.

In a **liquid**, particles are a little farther apart.

In a **gas**, particles are the farthest apart. Sound travels slowest through gases.

Answer these questions about how sound travels.

1. Which medium has particles that are very close together?

   _____

2. Which medium has particles that are the farthest apart?

   _____

3. If you make a sound, in which matter will the sound move fastest?

   _____

4. Will sound move fastest through a wood block, a swimming pool, or air? Explain

   _____

How do light and matter interact?

Materials can be grouped by how they react to light.

Letting Light Through

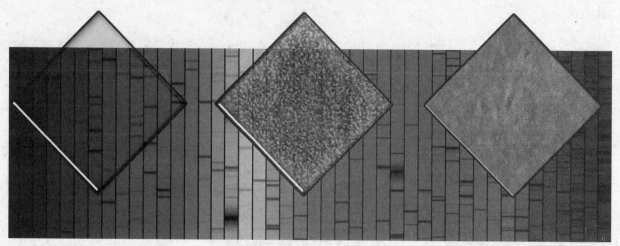

Transparent materials let almost all light rays pass through them.

Translucent materials let some light rays pass through them.

Opaque materials do not let any light rays pass through them.

Answer these questions about light and matter.

1. Which type of material lets almost all light through it?

   _____

2. Which type of material does not let any light rays pass through it?

   _____

3. Which type of material lets some light pass through?

   _____

4. Pretend you are looking through a sheet of waxed paper. Is waxed paper, transparent, translucent, or opaque? How do you know?

   _____

5. What is an example of an opaque material in your classroom?

   _____

What is motion?

Words like up, down, north, south, left, and right can be used to describe direction, but motion may be in straight lines, curved paths, or back and forth. Motion can also be measured using speed, which measures how fast an object moves.

The roller coaster slows down at the top of the loop.

The roller coaster reaches its greatest speed at the bottom of the loop.

The roller coaster slows down as it moves uphill.

The roller coaster moves in different directions.
The roller coaster also moves at different speeds.

Answer these questions.

1. At what point is the roller coaster moving the fastest?

_____

2. How can you describe the direction of the roller coaster as it moves around the loop?

_____

3. How can you describe the motion of the roller coaster?

_____

4. How can you describe the speed of the roller coaster when it starts to move uphill?

_____

5. What happens to the speed of the roller coaster as it moves down the loop?

_____

What are some types of stored energy?

Stored energy is potential energy. Potential energy can change into kinetic energy. Kinetic energy is the energy of motion.

Changing Types of Energy		
Types of Stored Energy	**How the Energy Is Used**	
Fossil fuels store potential energy from the Sun.	Fossil fuels burn to give vehicles kinetic energy.	
Plants store potential energy from the Sun.	The energy is released to support the animals that eat the plants.	
The water behind a dam has potential energy.	A hydroelectric power plant produces electric energy.	

Use the chart to answer the questions.

1. Which types of stored energy come from the Sun?

   _____

2. How can the potential energy from water behind a dam be used?

   _____

3. How is the stored energy in plants used?

   _____

4. What has to happen to the stored energy in fossil fuels to create kinetic energy?

   _____

Name _____

What is a complex machine?

A can opener is a complex machine with many smaller parts that are simple machines. The simple machines work together. *Complex* means "having many parts."

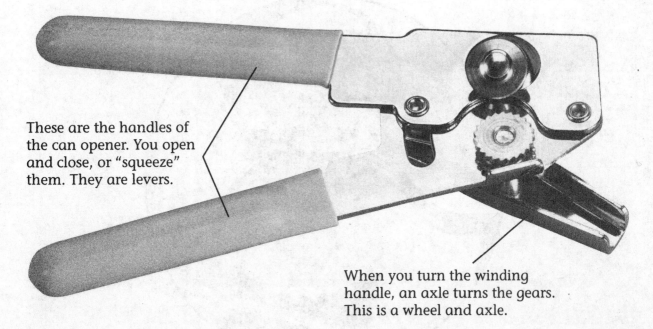

These are the handles of the can opener. You open and close, or "squeeze" them. They are levers.

When you turn the winding handle, an axle turns the gears. This is a wheel and axle.

Answer these questions.

1. What part of the can opener is a lever?

   _____

2. What type of simple machine is the winding handle on the can opener?

   _____

3. How does the winding handle make it easier to open a can?

   _____

4. What is a complex machine? How can you describe it?

   _____

   _____

What simple machines are part of complex machines?

The sharp edge that you use to cut into the top of the can is a wedge. A wheel that has spikes is a gear. The spikes are called teeth.

Answer these questions about the picture above.

1. What are the spikes on the bottom wheel called?

   _____

2. The top wheel has a sharp edge. What type of simple machine is it?

   _____

3. Tell where each simple machine in a can opener is found.

   _____

   _____

Name _____

What is Earth's orbit?

Earth spins. As it rotates, Earth follows a path around the Sun called an orbit. Earth's orbit is an ellipse. An ellipse is like a circle stretched out in opposite directions. During its orbit, Earth's axis is always tilted in the same direction. However, Earth's distance from the Sun changes. When the North Pole tilts toward the Sun, the Northern Hemisphere gets more direct sunlight. When the North Pole tilts away from the Sun, the Southern Hemisphere gets more direct sunlight.

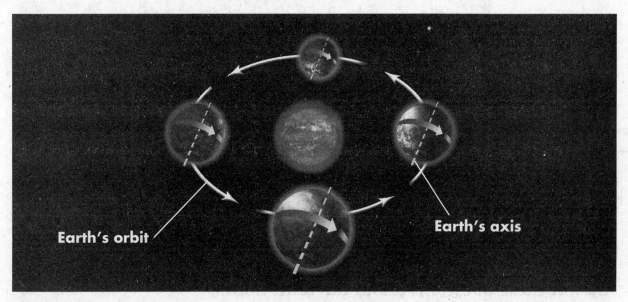

Earth's orbit

Earth's axis

Answer these questions about Earth's orbit.

1. Earth's orbit is an ellipse. What is an ellipse?

_____

2. What do the dotted lines on the picture show?

_____

3. What happens to the Southern Hemisphere when the Northern Hemisphere tilts toward the Sun?

_____

4. What do the white arrows on the picture show?

_____

5. Describe the direction of the tilt of Earth's axis during its orbit.

_____

How do the number of daylight hours change throughout the year?

The number of daylight hours every place on Earth, except at the equator, changes during the year. The graph below shows the number of daylight hours in one day for a city in the Northern Hemisphere.

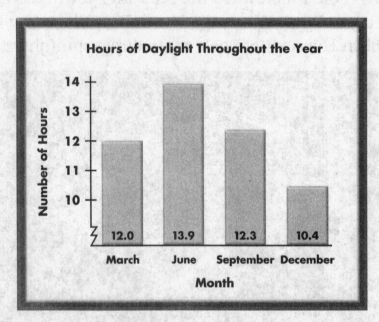

Answer these questions about daylight hours.

1. What does the column of numbers along the left side of the chart show?

   _____

2. How many hours of daylight were there in March?

   _____

3. In which month did the city receive 12.3 hours of daylight?

   _____

4. How did the hours of daylight change from June to December?

   _____

5. In which month did the city receive the fewest hours of daylight?

   _____

Workbook

What is in our solar system?

A planet is a large, ball-shaped object that moves around a star. In our solar system, planets orbit around the Sun. Our solar system has two groups of planets: the inner and outer planets. The inner planets are Mercury, Venus, Earth, and Mars. The outer planets are Jupiter, Saturn, Uranus, Neptune, and Pluto.

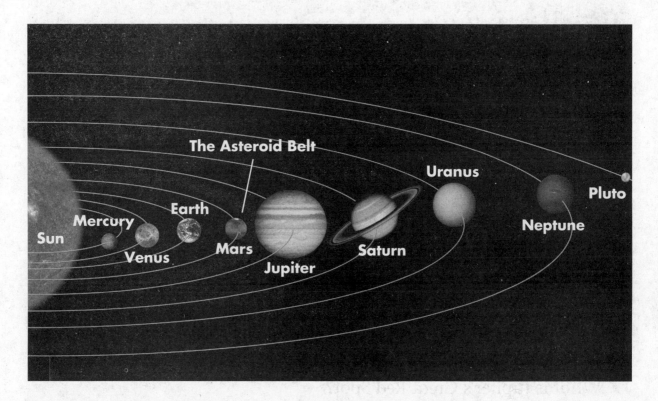

Answer these questions about the picture above.

1. How many planets orbit the Sun in our solar system? _____

2. Which planets are between the Sun and Earth? _____

3. What is found between the inner planets and the outer planets in the solar system? _____

4. What is the smallest outer planet? _____

5. What is the largest outer planet? _____

What is Jupiter?

Jupiter's **bands of clouds** make it a colorful object in the solar system.

Io is one of Jupiter's moons. Io has more active volcanoes than any other object in the solar system.

Europa is one of Jupiter's moons. Europa is very smooth. It has a frozen crust.

Ganymede is one of Jupiter's moons. Ganymede is the largest moon in the solar system.

The **Great Red Spot** is a weather system that has been raging for hundreds of years.

Callisto is one of Jupiter's moons. Callisto has more craters than any other object in the solar system.

Answer these questions about the picture above.

1. What is Jupiter's Great Red Spot?

   _____

2. What makes Jupiter such a colorful object in the solar system?

   _____

3. Which of Jupiter's moons is the largest in the solar system?

   _____

4. Which of Jupiter's moons has the most active volcanoes in the solar system?

   _____

5. How are the surfaces of Europa and Callisto different?

   _____

How does technology help keep us healthy?

X-rays are shadow pictures. They can find broken bones or tumors. Magnetic resonance imaging (MRI) technology can be used to learn about things that don't show up on X-rays.

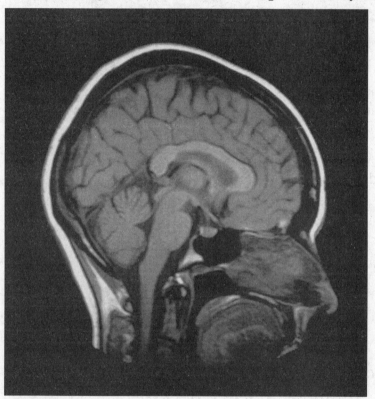

MRI Brain Scan

Teeth X-ray

Answer these questions.

1. What are X-rays?

   _____

2. What is magnetic resonance imaging (MRI) technology used for?

   _____

3. What does the X-ray above show?

   _____

4. What does the MRI picture show?

   _____

How have forms of communication changed?

In 1455, Johannes Gutenberg invented letter blocks that were used to print materials. Printing brought the benefits of writing to a wider group.

The electric telegraph was the earliest form of telecommunication. An electric current shot along a wire in short bursts called Morse code.

A quill is a hollow shaft of a feather. It was first used as a pen in A.D. 600.

Early video cameras took moving pictures and could also play them back.

Answer these questions about the forms of communication above.

1. What was the benefit of printing with letter blocks?

_____

2. What is a quill? What were quills used for?

_____

3. How did the electric telegraph work?

_____

_____

4. Who invented letter blocks?

_____

5. What was the earliest form of telecommunication?

_____

Picture Credits

Notes